did think I was Gemini with Scorpio rising. I've actually found out that I'm Gemini with Libra rising, but actually I think she might be right.

xx starstruck

Dear Starstruck

I love Debbie Harry more than I can ever properly put into words. She stood in the mosh pit watching my band Angelfish support The Ramones at The Academy in NY back in 1993 . She has graced many a Garbage show with her presence for years. For this, and for many other kindnesses she has extended to me over the years, I would fight lions with my bare hands for that woman. However I cannot side with her on this particular subject. I don't believe in starsigns. Not really. For example, everyone who meets me assumes I'm a Leo. Well, I'm not. I'm a Virgo, go figure. So fuck all that shit, my little starstruck friend. You're going to get on that road and you're going to make it your bitch. And when you are done you are going to look back and smile and think to yourself, "God bless you Debbie Harry. You are one of the greatest living icons of the 20th and the 21st Century but hell girl, you don't know SHIT about starsigns."

Yours truly, in agony
Auntie Beat

Dear Shirley,

When it comes to matters south of the border, I'm having an existential crisis: to muff, or not to muff?

Yours, Hairy McLairy

Dear Hairy McLairy

Personally I am not a fan of the non-existent muff myself. Quite frankly I am deeply suspicious of any man or woman who likes their cunt to look exactly like that of a newly birthed baby or a Barbie doll. It reeks of someone who is desperately immature or, worse still, hints at something dark and abhorrent. All things to avoid in matters pertaining to the sexual organs, if you ask me.

That said, I think the hedges must be kept trimmed. Overgrown ivy is also known to encourage creepy, dark and unwanted guests.

Yours truly, in agony
Auntie Beat

You have bigger fish to fry, surely? And feel good about being a weirdo. In this crazy, upside down, chaotic world of ours, you might as well face it. You fit right in.

Your truly, in agony
Auntie Beat

Dear Shirley

Every night my cat wakes me up at 4.20am by scratching the sofa until I feed her and then boot her outside. If I don't feed her she just scratches the door. We are all knackered, even the other cat has taken to sleeping under the wardrobe for a good nights kip. Should we get a dog?

Yours, Mz Kitty

Dear Mz Kitty

Should you get a dog? No. You absolutely should NOT. You can't even figure out how to keep a kitty, Mz Kitty. Incase you don't know this already, there actually is no such thing as a "naughty" animal. They generally want to fall in line with the household routine. You have to look in the mirror if your animal is exhibiting strange disruptive behaviour. You need to figure out what it is that YOU are doing wrong. The fault lies entirely at the feet of the human in charge. So why the 4:20am scratching, munching, peeing or shitting? How the fuck should I know? My natural inclination would be to seek advice from your local vet who, if worth their bloody salt, should be able to set you and by default your kitty on the straight.

Sorry for swearing.
Yours truly, in agony
Auntie Beat

SHIRLEY

punk perfect awful

punk perfect awful

beat: the little magazine that could... and did.

hanna hanra

RIZZOLI
NEW YORK

New York · Paris · London · Milan

contents

brian may's underpants

It's a balmy day in Los Angeles. The palm trees gently sway high above me in the blue sky. I open the door to the balcony of my hotel room, letting some warm air swirl around. The room stinks because it's on the smoking floor of the Sunset Marquis, a hotel on Sunset Boulevard that has been here since time began. The Label got me up here. Everyone refers to them as "The Label" and although I know that The Label is actually a multi-armed, multi-faceted conglomerate, I imagine it as a Wizard of Oz-type situation: one slightly frazzled older man shielding himself behind a tatty curtain, pumping levers and pulleys as horses change colour on a whim and everyone high-kicks around him, working out release dates and B-sides and tour schedules.

The hotel is fabulously scuzzy. It is where The Label puts young bands who are passing through town to sign a deal or going into the studio or playing a showcase. Those young bands often graduate to being part of the musical canon; sometimes, they don't. That boozy, young energy isn't the only thing seeping out of the zebra-print carpet. The décor hasn't been touched since 1970—or 1980, or 1990, it's hard to tell. I light a cigarette on the balcony and survey my surroundings. The balcony overlooks the pool; no-one is swimming. I haven't brought my swimsuit, and anyway, that's not what I am here for.

It's 2010. There's no social media to immortalise the moment, there's barely a camera phone. The night before, after I'd landed and had a shower, I got dressed and walked six blocks down the street, jay-walked over the road at Liquor Locker and walked back. I ate two tacos from that truck opposite the Chateau Marmont and just felt so excited, like the world was suddenly so rich with colour.

Dave Grohl's manager meets me at the hotel reception and we get into her car. Whatever she's used to make her hair curly makes the car smell coconutty and sweet, a refreshing change from the hotel room, and although she asks me a thousand questions about the music I just started, I try to keep my eyes pointed out of the window as we drive to his house. I don't tell her that I work out of a basement in grubby old Dalston, a dumpster of a neighbourhood in East London, or that I'm just making it up as I go along and have no idea how I've swung an interview with Dave Grohl for the second issue. I want to drink in every detail of where we are, every weirdo on the sidewalk, every overflowing trash can, every billboard, and every cloud of pollution on the freeway.

*

I am six years old in the back of my parents' car and, with a satisfying clunk, I press play on my Walkman. The foam headphones haven't left my ears since it was given to me—a month of negotiating and begging and good behaviour, and this is my reward. A wee black box that will shape my life. I peer out the window; outside is wintery grey Scotland and bare trees slip past as we drive home, but that's outside so it doesn't matter because inside my head "Bohemian Rhapsody." I have exactly one cassette that Mum's friend gave me; on one side is written Queen's Greatest Hits in blue Biro and on the other it says Hits of the 1960s. "Bohemian Rhapsody" is the first song I hear, just because that's where the tape starts, and it blows my mind every time I hear it. The way it starts gently with a question, before blowing into full dramatics that make me want to move every atom of my body. It reshapes my brain. I love it. I love the high notes and the guitar, and how it sounds so different to the guitar on the Dire Straits album Mum plays constantly. I hate Dire Straits and turn the volume down when she's not looking—they sound so boring and angry at the world, not like my beloved Freddie Mercury, who can not only sing like a lady, but also makes ladies seem so exciting. Dire Straits do not sing about fat-bottomed girls making the world go round. Dire Straits do not make music that is exciting to me.

Queen are pure fantasy to me, and through their music I understand that there is a world much bigger than the one I live in. I've never experienced the anticipation of meeting a lover at the Ritz at 9pm for dinner, or buying the wine. I don't know what a Killer Queen is, but she sounds fascinating, like the most glamorous and brilliant woman, and I decide on the spot that when I grow up I want to be dynamite with a laser beam, too. I want to be on the cassette, and I learn every word to every song on the cassette, and when the Queen side is finished, I simply rewind it and play it again.

...

The black gates of Dave Grohl's house swing open and Gaby parks the car. Dave is standing in the doorway holding a coffee cup, he says something to Gaby and ushers me into his studio through a white door in the hallway. It's the garage to his house, filled with kit, guitars, drums, a mixing desk. He gestures to me to sit in an office chair, one of those that spin round, and I do, tippy-toeing it round to face the giant mixing desk that takes up most of the studio. Dave makes me promise that I'm not recording because he's going to play me his new album, Wasting Light, which he made right there in his garage / studio with Butch Vig. I know about Butch from years of judiciously reading liner notes in albums, together with every issue of the NME and MOJO. He produced Nirvana's Nevermind and is part of Garbage—two bands who coaxed me through my teenage years. I am so lost in thought about what it must be like to be Dave Grohl, while Dave Grohl is actually sitting there, playing me his new album, that I solidify. When the album is finished playing I turn the Dictaphone on.

Did you have to do a lot of soul searching?
Not really. I don't feel like I needed to get into a particular headspace or anything when I'm doing vocals, I guess. It's just a part of what I do. When we started writing all of this stuff, our bass player Nate sent me this email that said, "I really love this music that we're writing but I want you to know that it's OK to not take everything so seriously all the time." I don't think that most people consider The Foo Fighters to take ourselves too seriously, but sometimes when you're making an album, it's hard to feel lighthearted about anything because it's the most important thing in your life at the moment. So, he said, "You know, there are songs that you've written that I really love that are kind of funny. You don't have to sit down and try to write Blood On The Tracks or Imagine every time." And it was nice, it really lifted the weight off of my shoulders. There's this song called "White Limo."

"White Limo" used to be a sort of text code for getting really, really fucked up—that song's about nothing at all. I love it. There's a line in it that says, "Whatever happened to day-glo thongs"—and that's why it's easy to scream, because I don't feel like I have to write a love letter to myself. Actually, there was a song that was gonna be on this album that we've been trying to record for thirteen years.

Really? What made you want to record it now?
Well, we haven't put it on the record. Do you like how we've hung Brian May's underwear on the record this time then it wouldn't come out.

Do you want it to come out?
No. That's why we haven't put it on. Do you like how we've hung Brian May's underwear over the door like mistletoe?

I look up. Above the door is a pair of mossy-green men's Y-fronts pinned to the wall with thumbtacks.

Which do you prefer, being at the front or playing the drums?
I prefer both. When I'm tired of being the front man of the band and playing in front of thousands of people I go back to being the drummer and the guy that isn't at the front of the band. They are both the biggest responsibilities in the band. Without a great drummer you don't have a great band, without a great front person you don't have a great band. Imagine Queen with a different lead singer. Would I have their guitarist's underwear hanging on my wall? Probably not. What if Led Zeppelin had a shitty drummer? It's unimaginable. I actually have two Queen fanatics in the band. Taylor and Pat Smear. Pat was, like, stalking Freddie at the Sunset Marquis in like,1975.

Brian played on this record, didn't he?
Yeah. So Brian came down to play on the record, he shows up at the studio, he's wearing these running shorts and black socks and sneakers, and he has two huge bags from Amoeba records. So, he puts the bags down and says, "I'm going to change my clothes," and he comes back in, in these like MC Hammer pants. And he plays the lead, and he hangs out and then he had to split. He called like an hour later and said, "You guys, I left one of my bags in the room, just leave it in there, I'll come back and get it." So I was like, "OK." and hung up the phone and looked in there... He never came to get his bag. Do you want to touch them?

***

Back in my hotel room that evening, I lie full of jet lag on the bed, my eyes wide open. I think about reaching up and touching the gusset of Brian May's pants, and Freddie Mercury at the bar downstairs in 1975. He was right here. Did he do cocaine from this bedside table? They were just ordinary pants. Pinned above a garage door, I shut my eyes and a sound floats into my head. A clunk. A pause. A falsetto. *Is this the real life? Is this just fantasy?*

And then I realise something. I still have never listened to the second side of that goddam cassette.

ISSUE 32 AW2022 FREE!

FLOWEROVLOVE BY THOMAS CRISTIANI

Issue 20, Autumn Winter 2016   free!   thebeatjuice.com

GOAT GIRL photographed by Angelo Pennetta

thebeatjuice.com   FREE!

Issue 27, Spring Summer 2019

These New Puritans by Angelo Pennetta

Bobby Gillespie by Angelo Pennetta

GOSSIP GRIMES KINDNESS KURT COBAIN FREE

GARBAGE SANTIGOLD JESSIE WARE SHUGA

PANDA BEAR FRIENDS GIRLS TOY

JE #4 LONDON SPRING/SUMMER 2012

LUKE, ZULU, PHOTOGRAPHY BY ALASDAIR MCLELLAN

THEBEATJUICE.COM

BY FELIX COOPER

ISSUE 30 WINTER 2021 FREE

Georgia photographed by Letty Schmiterlow

Issue 23, Winter 2017 free! thebeatjuice.com

Jenny Lee Lindberg: "If you had told me that someday Sonic Youth would like our band or even know I existed at all, I wouldn't have known what to say." - Warpaint, issue 1

of youth. "The role of youth doesn't matter, and it hasn't ch
to snarl down the phone. "Whether it's the 1950s, the 60s, the
whatever, you just need to live and find the good people and ke
We haven't seen youth gather for a while and maybe it won
be they'll grow even more pale and dead instead of getting stro
22-year-old sounds like he wants to fill the role of the angry pro
voice of his people. Does it matter to him, the disparate youth?
bothered about it," he says, quickly becoming disinterested. Al
the band, Johan Surrballe Wieth, Dan Kjær Nielsen and Jakob
produce clever and archaic music. It is combative, sitting sou

to Woodstock, where he died. Wally Hope was arrested for possession... them, in fact, sectioned. He died of asphyxiation on his own vomit fro... many sleeping pills. But, unlike his muddled heroes, Elias sees a prosp... very much considering Teenage "a long term project." He's not in any... though. "It will happen when it happens," he says, sounding reflectiv... to keep developing in a natural way, we're like a little seed that grows... flower. So, who knows."

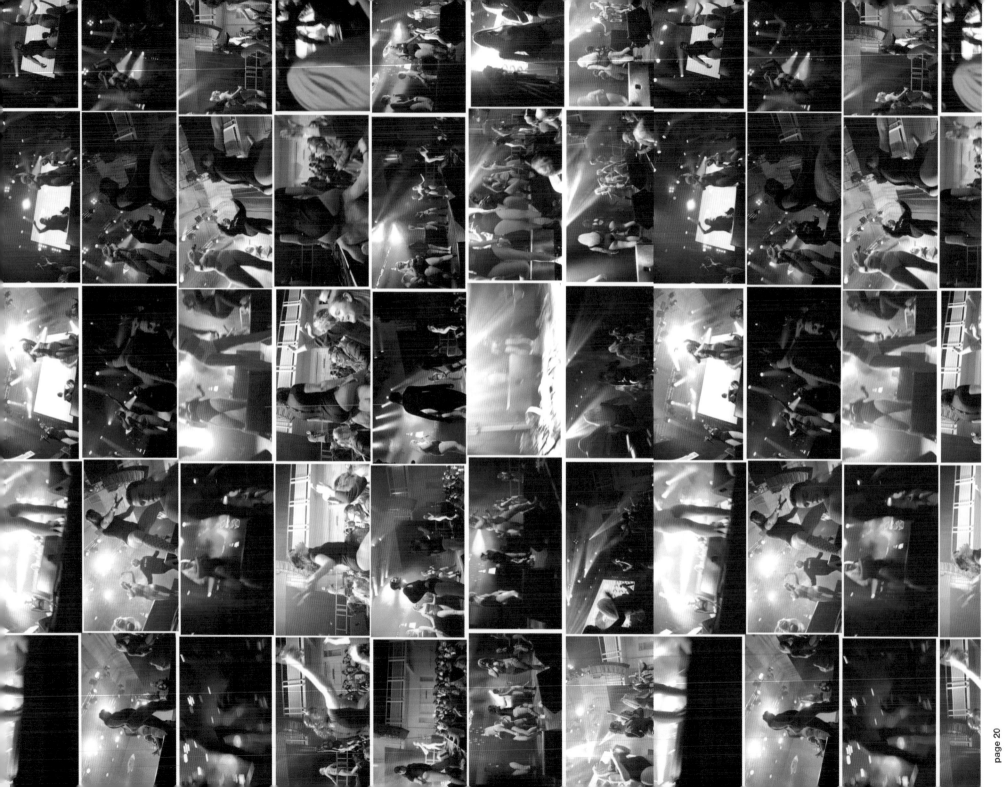

KATHLEEN HANNA, ISSUE 25

When did you first consider yourself to be a musician?

I did the first Julie Ruin record as Bikini Kill were falling apart. I guess that was 1998. And then *Le Tigre* came out in 1999. And that was the time. In Bikini Kill, I thought of myself as a feminist performance artist who played someone in a band, and that's what gave me so much freedom to be confrontational. I thought I was bringing performance art into punk music, and also talking about feminism and violence against women. I felt like I was an outreach worker, and a big part of what I was writing was to kids who were having a hard time and didn't have anyone to turn to. I'm really proud of what we did. Then, when I started working on my own project, I started hearing what I wanted to make. I learned how to use a sampler and play keyboards and guitar.

I taught myself how to do all these things because I just wanted to sing and needed something to sing with, and to expect all this stuff to not hold myself back with "you have to write 'Rebel Girl' again." I just wrote about what I was feeling at the time, which was a lot of sadness and frustration. But I was really in love at the time and I wrote a for-real love song, which was weird because it makes me really happy, it brings me back to that time.

When did you realise you were a role model?

When I was returning people's letters I realised I could help, because I'd had training as a sexual assault counsellor. It was just one person writing to another but at the same time, I knew what stuff to stay. One of my main things was trying to get people to get help. Just encouraging people to get local help and not just writing to a singer from some random band. You just need to know you're not alone. But I never felt like I was a role model, I just felt like I was using my counselling skills.

What about Riot Grrrl?

When people focused on me as the face of Riot Grrrl and a role model, it was like, "What?" At the time I was, like, a stripper. And I needed to be myself and do what I needed to do. I don't want to lie about things or come off as being perfect and not making mistakes. I don't think stripping was a mistake at all and I don't look back at it and feel devastated or like my life was ruined. I was just confused by that role. And in a way, who could want a better role model than a punk-rock stripper with sexual abuse training? For me it didn't feel like I was punk rock at all. I just had to make money so we could get the tour bus repaired and go on tour. There was no other job I could have done that would have enabled me to pay my way through college. I hunted and hunted but none would hire me. It was a big moment of independence but it was also really degrading. I'm just really happy now that I have a job that I love.

"You know them 'F-you' songs? That was probably my first instance of writing. But in my head I wasn't writing, I guess it was journaling." - Debbie, issue 32

photographed by Angelo Pennetta in London

SUGABABES, ISSUE 29

Is it weird when new artists tell you that One Touch inspired them?

MUTYA: No. Not really.

KEISHA: Oh, for me it is! When Stormzy was like, "Oh my gosh, a Sugababe." I was like, "You know me?" It throws you off when he said things like, "I remember you guys from primary school days." Jorja Smith, people like that. They definitely remind you of how old you are.

What message would you give to your younger selves starting the journey twenty years ago if you could?

MUTYA: I'd say to appreciate things a bit more. A lot of things seem like a blur to me.

KEISHA: Enjoy it more, but also be myself more. I would have been in therapy from a lot younger so I could embrace things a bit more. Or a of the things we did with "Flatline," when we shot the video in Malibu, we walked to the edge of the sea and we took a second. I was like, "Let's just take this all in."

SIOBHAN: I remember you saying that, it was so lovely.

KEISHA: Things just go so quickly and then it's finished. It always seems so stressful and so big, but you have to enjoy it because it doesn't last forever.

SIOBHAN: It's easier in hindsight, right, but just to be less hard on ourselves. As Keisha said, just to enjoy the moment. To bring more empathy to the table. Everyone's got their own stuff going on.

BEAT

FREE

#6 SPRING 2013

"I: was always women who didn't seem to care, ⊤hat's who I was drawn to." - Romy, The xx, issue 5

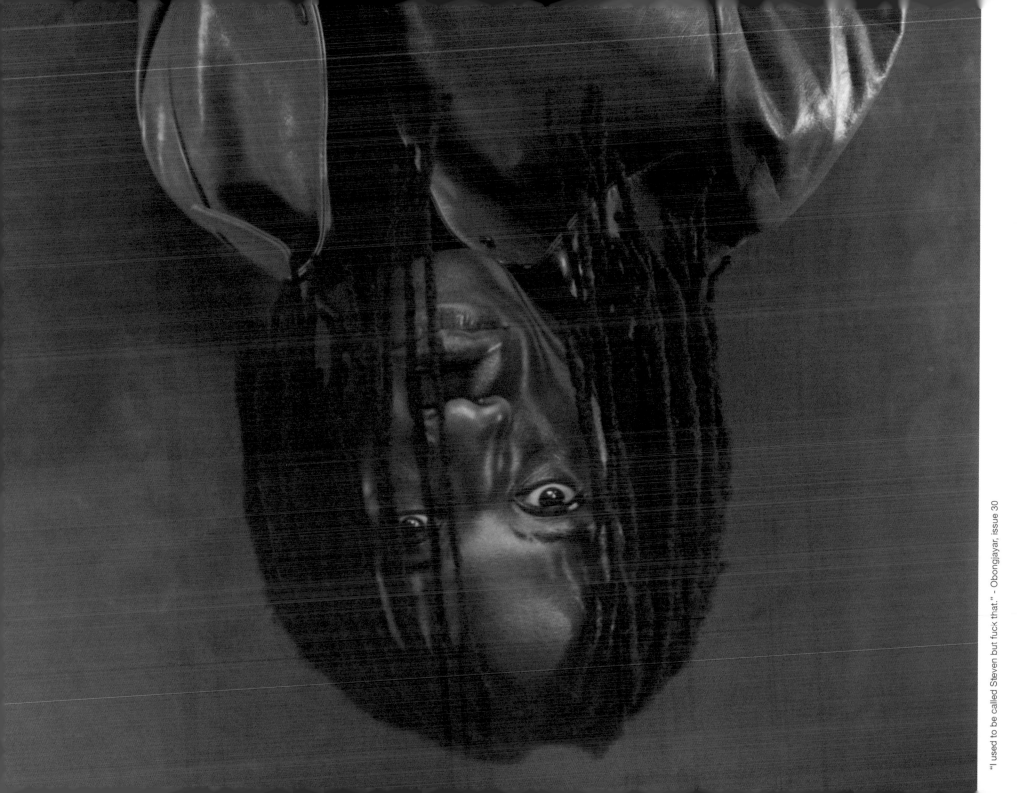

Vagabon
by *Chad Moore*
for issue 28
spring 2019

Zebra Katz
by *Rafael Rios*
for issue 5
winter 2012

Brett Anderson
by *Clare Shilland*
for issue 2
spring 2011

Wolf Alice
by *Jack Davison*
for issue 7
summer 2013

Yak
by *Angelo Pennetta*
for issue 26
winter 2018

Sky Ferreira
by *Letty Schmiterlow*
for issue 6
spring 2013

Diiv
by *Ryan McGinley*
for issue 6
spring 2013

The XX
by *Alasdair McLellan*
for issue 5
autumn 2012

Obongjayar
by *Bolade Banjo*
for issue 30
winter 2021

Warpaint
by *Clare Shilland*
for issue 1
winter 2010

Thrush Metal
by *Tyrone Lebon*
for issue 1
winter 2010

Deb Never
by *Lewis Vorn*
for issue 30
winter 2021

Flo
by *Lillie Eiger*
for issue 31
spring 2022

Daughters of Reykjavik
by *Andrea Björk*
for issue 24
winter 2017

Eraserheads
by *Alasdair McLellan*
for issue 1
winter 2010

NTS Radio
by *Tyrone Lebon*
for issue 4
winter 2011

Role Model
by *Khufu Nahjee*
for issue 31
summer 2022

Sunflower Bean
by *Chad Moore*
for issue 31
summer 2022

Debbie
by *Bolade Banjo*
for issue 32
winter 2022

Goat Girl
by *Angelo Pennetta*
for issue 20
winter 2016

Miguel
by *Max Farago*
for issue 15
summer 2015

These New Puritans
by *Angelo Pennetta*
for issue 27
summer 2019

Goat Girl
by *Angelo Pennetta*
for issue 20
winter 2016

Zulu
by *Alasdair McLellan*
for issue 4
summer 2012

Georgia
by *Letty Schmiterlow*
for issue 24
winter 2017

Bobby Gillespie
by *Angelo Pennetta*
for issue 18
spring 2016

Flowerovlove
by *Thomas Cristiani*
for issue 32
winter 2022

Deem Spencer
by *Frank Lebon*
for issue 24
spring 2018

Lil Nas X
by *Felix Cooper*
for issue 30
winter 2021

Warpaint
by *Clare Shilland*
for issue 1
winter 2010

Charli XCX
by *Chad Mocre*
for issue 21
summer 2017

Panda Bear
by *Michael Hauptman*
for issue 4
summer 2012

Ice Age
by *Letty Schmiterlow*
for issue 7
summer 2013

TRANSFORMER

BEAT

£ $ ¥ Free
Vol 2 No 2   THEBEATJUICE.COM

PERFUME GENIUS Photographed by DREW JARRETT Autumn 2014   + JESSIE WARE / KING TUFF / ARCA / IBEYI / MNEK +

absolute beginners

I'm in a nightclub in London in 2003 and I overhear the promoter saying he's looking for DJs. I tell him that I am one—it seems easy enough, and I feel like it might a good way to meet people, in many different senses of the word. Looking back, it was a spur-of-the-moment decision that has paid for itself a million times over. Not because I once DJed on a boat next to Grace Jones, who sang a full set wearing only a belly chain and a hat, but because I got to explore my true love, which, as should be obvious by now, is music.

Deciding to start BEAT was also a spur-of-the-moment decision. It just seemed like A Great Idea. What could possibly go wrong? Starting a magazine, with no experience of starting a magazine, in a basement in Dalston, with no money and only a few valiant friends roped in to help? I knew that it had to be a specific size—large—so I found the one printer in all of the United Kingdom that could print at the right size. I called them and the guy at the end of the line sounded unsure whether they could print 88 pages and staple them together, but I guessed he would figure it out. What was great about this extra-large size I had demanded the magazine be, was that you could make the pictures really big. And that was what the magazine was about: really mega pictures of musicians and bands and artists and DJs that were big enough to rip out and stick on your wall.

In 2010, the music magazine waters were very different. It was the tail end of a time when things were greasy and unregulated, make-up was applied with fingers, handbags were just simple cotton totes, the sort that are perfect for potatoes or your laptop, and would invariably be dumped on the floor of the bar. Jeans were still eye-wateringly tight and looking after yourself meant having a burger after drinking in the bar all night. On one hand, a very liberated time, free from doing anything to please anyone other than yourself, but on the other, a time when being a woman, or being gay, or being different and not fitting into the mould, was a hindrance, not a help. I had stopped DJing because I realised I would never be the top of the bill—not because I wasn't good enough, but because promoters just never booked chicks to headline. I was also sick of being asked by sound men if I knew what I was doing.

One of my favourite things about DJing was that there are certain songs that everyone just loses their shit to, and then you get the pleasure of chasing it up with a song they maybe haven't heard, could be new, could be old. It's something you've discovered and you want to share. I love that. I loved watching people dance to a demo of Late Of The Pier, or a song by an unsigned band called The xx that I'd ripped off their Myspace. So I would make BEAT like a record collection, or a playlist. A little bit of everything all rolled into one. But especially musicians who weren't four white guys in a band. Not that there's anything wrong with four white guys in a band, but it was time to let everyone else have a moment in the sun. The idea behind BEAT was that if you liked something you found on one page, you might like the musician you found on the next, so it wouldn't matter if they were the biggest musician in the world or a group of refugees, like Songhoy Blues, a band who escaped Sharia Law in Mali only to record an album with Nick Zinner of the Yeah Yeah Yeahs.

The other thing about BEAT, I decided, was that the pictures had to stand the test of time. In 2010, the music press was really divided into two genres: Blokes In Bands Down Brick Lane Against A Wall, or Girls In Fashion Magazines (they had to be really famous though). I remembered a quote from my favourite philosopher, David Bowie—"you hear what you see"—and one of the things I've loved about all the musicians I've ever loved (and there have been a few) is that they are all so cool. Why would you drag them down Brick Lane or shoehorn them into clothes so that they don't look like themselves, or how they want to be seen on stage or on their record? So it was written into stone / onto a note and stuck to the wall that BEAT would shoot people looking like how they look. Now I had the basic tenets of my magazine: A great name, a premise on how people would look, a motto about who to include, lightly probing journalism, and a gung-ho attitude toward financial modelling and printing. We were off.

Although we shot actual icon Nick Cave for the first issue, it was so clear to me that Warpaint had to be on the cover. I'd discovered them on a CD my friend had given me of indie covers of Bowie songs. They'd

recorded a particularly delicious version of Ashes to Ashes. Clare Skilland shot the most beautiful picture of Theresa Wayman and Jenny Lee Lindberg back to back. Theresa's long hair contrasting with Jenny Lee's shaved head. I knew it would make a great cover. The image said everything that I wanted the magazine to say: it felt new and uncompromising and beautiful, but it wasn't objectifying anyone.

We printed it on the big paper, and it arrived at our "office" in tightly wrapped bundles in the middle of a snowstorm. My friends and I lugged them into the tiny office, piling them high above our heads and then cracking the plastic strapping open to ogle each issue as if it were a brand-new baby. We were jubilant. The grumpy printer had done a sterling job, nothing was missing or lo-res, and there weren't too many spelling mistakes. A triumph! The large print size turned out to be a blessing and a curse—it looked great, but it did not fit in any envelope known to mankind, so each issue had to be sent as a parcel, which was expensive.

I still love that cover. It really captures a moment but it also feels so timeless. When I look at it now I can feel that moment, the crackle in time of hearing Warpaint's debut single, "Undertow," and how it felt and sounded so unlike anything else I'd heard. I remember how it made me feel, like I was being drowned in hot tar—and loving it. A little after the magazine came out, the band were in London, playing the Scala, and invited me to come along. I got to hang out with them for a moment after one of their shows. They'd filled the venue. Afterwards, we went to a house party together, at Conan's from Conan and the Mockasins flat in Shoreditch. Several tequilas in, I have a vague memory of telling Jenny Lee that I loved her hair, so short with just the little wisps at the front to frame her face. She looked at me dead in the eyes and said, "You should do your hair like this, too." Suddenly there was a pair of clippers in her hand and she was shaving my hair right off, in the middle of Conan's living room. Before she'd worked her way through both sides of my head the clippers started to smoke and the smell of burning hair filled the party. She pulled away from my head and in that moment, I realised that not every spur-of-the-moment decision is a great one.

"There's part of me that just wants to be honest, and I feel like there's a lot of other people's music I enjoy where I really respect their honesty." - Sampha, issue 20

"Death has always been something that has bewildered me, in that we're all so terrified of it but it's the only thing that is certain." - Tendai, issue 30

NENEH CHERRY, ISSUE 25

What you did was so new. I have a friend who says, even now, every time he sees a girl in a shopping centre with the little backpack, the puffa jacket, the nails, the big earrings, the hightops, he can see how you changed culture.

We were just playing around with the things we liked, the things that we were into. It was the heyday of the hip-hop queens, Latifah, Roxanne Shante...

To take that New York Canal Street flavour and give it this British high-fashion elegance and humour was so visually potent.

We twisted it up. We didn't owe anyone. We were never supposed to do the right thing.

We flipped it over. But always just that thing of taking the scratchy and the even, taking a designer thing and putting it with a trainer. Putting a piece of trash on it. Who makes the rules? I don't understand what they are. Obviously, you have respect for other human beings, a basic border to recognise and practice to have a nicer life. But that concept of an order to material life? No.

Does your past seem real to you?

Honestly no, that's why I hang out, cling on so firmly to the actuality of the situation. When I'm performing, it's like, "What time, what day, where is it, what time, how long is the show and who will be playing with?" That's kind of the maximum connectivity I go to. The studio is a bit more fraught, you never know what's going to happen, but it's still a bit like that; where, when, who am I playing with, how long have we got, that kind of thing. I keep it down to that. The big stuff—other people see it, I don't. It's my life. It's what I live and as far as I know, that's what everybody's life is like. That's what I feel deep inside.

When you're living your life, it just seems like that's what you do, doesn't it?

Yeah, it's not such a big deal. When I lived on the street I could have gone back to my mother's in Berkshire easily if I'd been prepared to live with her and cope with that. And for two years I couldn't, and I had to leave and sort of hang out on the street, really. I suppose compared to bourgeois life it probably looks terrible, but of course what one is doing, when you do something like that, is trying to avoid bourgeois life.

How do you define success?

Well, success is enough money to live. I've got a lovely apartment in Paris and I've got a little house in County Waterford, which is all very nice. I've got really good friends and a wonderful son. And I think it's also really the ability to do more records.

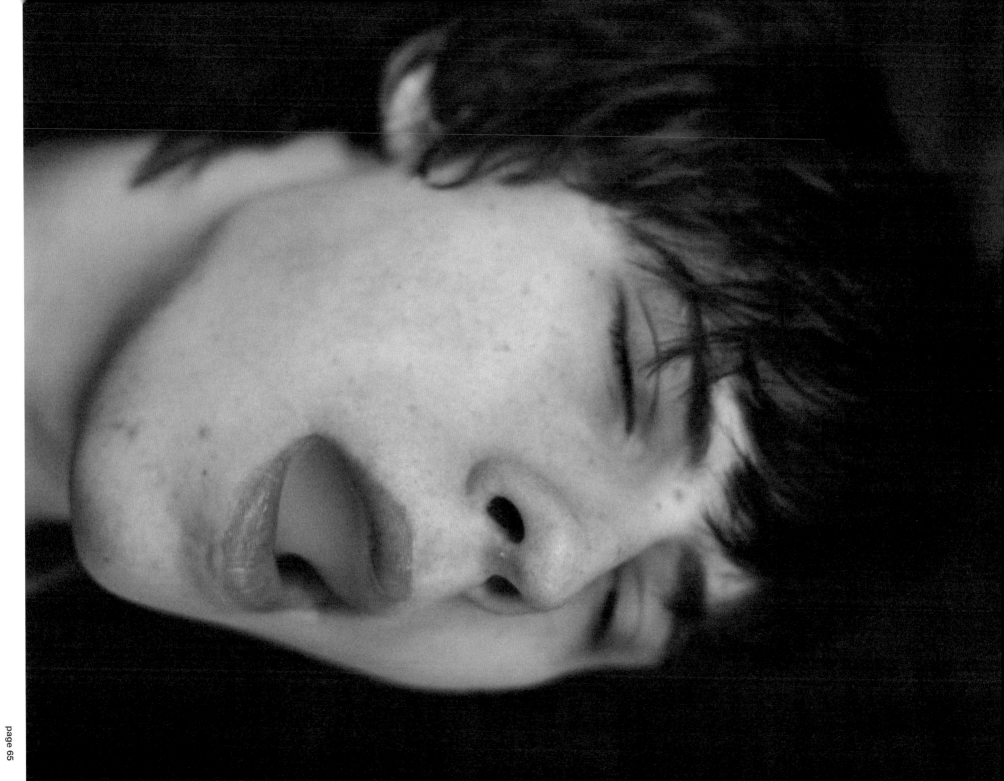

The Last Dinner Party
by *Clare Shilland*
for issue 32
winter 2022

Jake Bugg
by *Oliver Hadlee Pearch*
for issue 4
spring 2012

Last Night At Cordy House
by *Tyrone Lebon*
for issue 5
winter 2012

Devlin
by *Alasdair McLellan*
for issue 2
spring 2011

Perfume Genius
by *Drew Jarrett*
for issue 12
spring 2013

Shamir
by *Hobbes Ginsberg*
for issue 14
spring 2015

Sampha
by *Frank Lebon*
for issue 20
winter 2016

Tendai
by *Dexter Lander*
for issue 30
winter 2021

Tiana Major9
by *Grace Difford*
for issue 31
spring 2022

Throwing Up
by *Clare Shilland*
for issue 3
winter 2011

Bella Poarch
by *Sean Behr*
for issue 32
winter 2022

Petite Meller
by *Oliver Hadlee Pearch*
for issue 15
summer 2015

Mabel
by *Clare Shilland*
for issue 16
winter 2015

Yak
by *Errol Rainey*
for issue 18
winter 2016

Skinny Girl Diet
by *Clare Shilland*
for issue 14
spring 2015

Sampha
by *Frank Lebon*
for issue 20
winter 2016

BEAT

RAPTURE

DIIV BY RYAN McGINLEY

#6 SPRING 2013

FREE

THEBEATJUICE.COM

BEAT

ISSUE NO9 WINTER 2013/14

IZZI MANFREDI FROM THE PREATURES BY FELIX COOPER

The Preatures • Dev Hynes • Katy B • Phantasy • Drenge • Radky

FREE

THEBEATJUICE.COM

BEAT

JOSH, EUPHOBEAT, PHOTOGRAPHY BY ALASDAIR McLELLAN

ISSUE #1 LONDON WINTER 2010

FREE

THEBEATJUICE.COM

beat

Issue 25, Winter 2017   free   thebeatjuice.com

Kelela photographed by Lee Colombo

doing things for yourself
is a beautiful nightmare

(aka things i know now
but didn't know at the time)

A long, long time ago, when I started BEAT in a basement far away, I just wanted to edit a music magazine. Times were different then and this was not a job opportunity available for anyone outside of a small selection of people (you don't have to stretch your imagination very far to guess what sort of people I am talking about). So I, with no prior knowledge of running a magazine, or a business, decided that it was definitely something I could simply force into reality if I put my mind to it and called three printers to get the best quote. I met everyone I knew to tell them that I was going to launch a magazine. In some ways, this was to hold myself accountable because there is nothing worse than someone saying, "Oh, what about that thing you mentioned?" and your having to swiftly change the subject and reverse out the door. And in other ways, it was to sense check that it was a good idea. Some friends asked important questions that you hadn't thought of like, "How will you distribute it?"—and I'd reply, "Sure!" Inevitably I had not thought of how I would distribute it nor how I would pay for it, nor even if I knew any other writers. So, like any plucky young thing with time on her hands, I learned swiftly, by doing it myself. The first few issues were distributed via a friend's car that I drove at speed around London, bombing bundles of issues into unsuspecting shops before anyone could catch me and complain. I had no idea, really, how to set up a shoot or an interview, so I just made it up as I went along, badgering PRs for musicians' time and hoping for the best. And that is how I got Nick Cave in issue one and Adele in issue two.

This ad-hoc tactic led me on a journey of discovery. I discovered that sometimes things go wrong and you just have to go with it and, at the end of the day, only the people who know it's gone wrong will know. And most of the time, they won't remember later, anyway. I discovered that sometimes people can go out of their way to be lovely and kind, and sometimes they can go out of their way just to yank your teats for no particular reason. And when they do, you have to kill them.

(With kindness and patience, of course.)

I discovered that research is crucial if you don't want to embarrass yourself in front of your favourite musician, and that you should always be just a little bit early and never, for the love of God, late! Especially if it's your own magazine! Crucially, I discovered that if you start something with a wee bit of integrity and some love people will email you from around the world asking to be part of it, in one way or another—and then all of a sudden you have a thing. A community! Back in the basement, I never would have thought that anyone would ever tell me that they had BEAT on their walls, or collected it when they were younger, and now, here they are, excitedly shooting a cover for it. And how great is that?

But most importantly, I discovered that a list is a great editorial device.

A list of things that happened that I never thought would happen:

1. You will find yourself doing jobs that you never thought you'd find yourself doing. Jobs like cleaning up rat shit because someone left a packet of Ryvita open (justifiably, because it was you who did this), or chasing invoices, or designing a website, will suddenly become skills you possess. At some point you will not only find someone else to learn these skills, but also the knowledge of how to ask them to carry them out.

2. You will say yes to things that you don't know how to get out of.

3. You will say no to things that you wish you said yes to.

4. You will invent various *noms-de-plume* so that people don't know that you are the boss and the intern (may I introduce Annette Curtain and Thai Greene?).

5. Michael, who will join as Editor, will interview Geri Halliwell at her house. Her tiny, fluffy dog will secretly fart into his Dictaphone while he's interviewing her, and he will only hear it when he transcribes it later on. It's very small and bubbly and I will never not be funny.

6. You will interview high-brow art rockers via WhatsApp. You will do this because you know them on a personal level and because you are the boss and you're a tiny bit lazy at times.

7. You will get Paris Hilton to interview Charli XCX via WhatsApp because she too is the actual boss and she can do what she wants.

8. You will be so so so so surprised when Beyoncé asks to be on the cover, and you will have to give working on this cover the codename "Rachel Stevens," because every time you say it, it doesn't seem real (and because you signed an NDA).

9. You will be more surprised when David Bowie asks if he can, too.

10. You will make many, many friends along the way, from musicians to writers and photographers and publicists.

11. You will probably make a couple of enemies, too.

12. It's possible that you jumped from issue 10 to issue 12—there's no proof of issue 11 anywhere. It's an unlucky number anyway.

13. You will print every issue of the magazine with at least one clanger of a spelling mistake. And you will not car.

14. You will encourage your friend, an artist of note, to hide in the toilets of the Tate Modern, with only a small packet of KP peanuts for sustenance, only to come out after six hours to watch Kraftwerk, because they have not managed to get a ticket.

15. You have the absolute privilege to see more live music than you thought imaginable. Some that you adore and who shaped you and some who are new to the world. Some will be etched into your memory and some will be long forgotten. Either way, lucky you.

16. You will learn that sometimes the best ideas are the ones that come to you last minute, in a rush, and are pulled off in a panic.

17. You will put a lot of faith in people and they will rarely let you down.

18. You will be profoundly moved, sometimes, by the stuff musicians come out with when you interview them, and it will carry you through life.

19. But sometimes musicians tell you that "if you had any idea of style, you'd understand us a bit better," or that love smells "of cock."

20. And sometimes you will wonder just what the fuck they're on about.

BEAT

Oh Sheezus!

BEAT

The Pioneers: The xx

photographed by Alasdair McLellan

BEAT

The Hit Machine: Charli XCX

photographed by Chad Moore

That's hot

BEAT

FREE

Do you feel older than 23? "Yeah, I certainly do. But sometimes I feel like I'm about 5, so it's a weird balance. It's like, 'am I a 10-year-old boy or a 60-year-old woman?'" – Sky Ferreira,

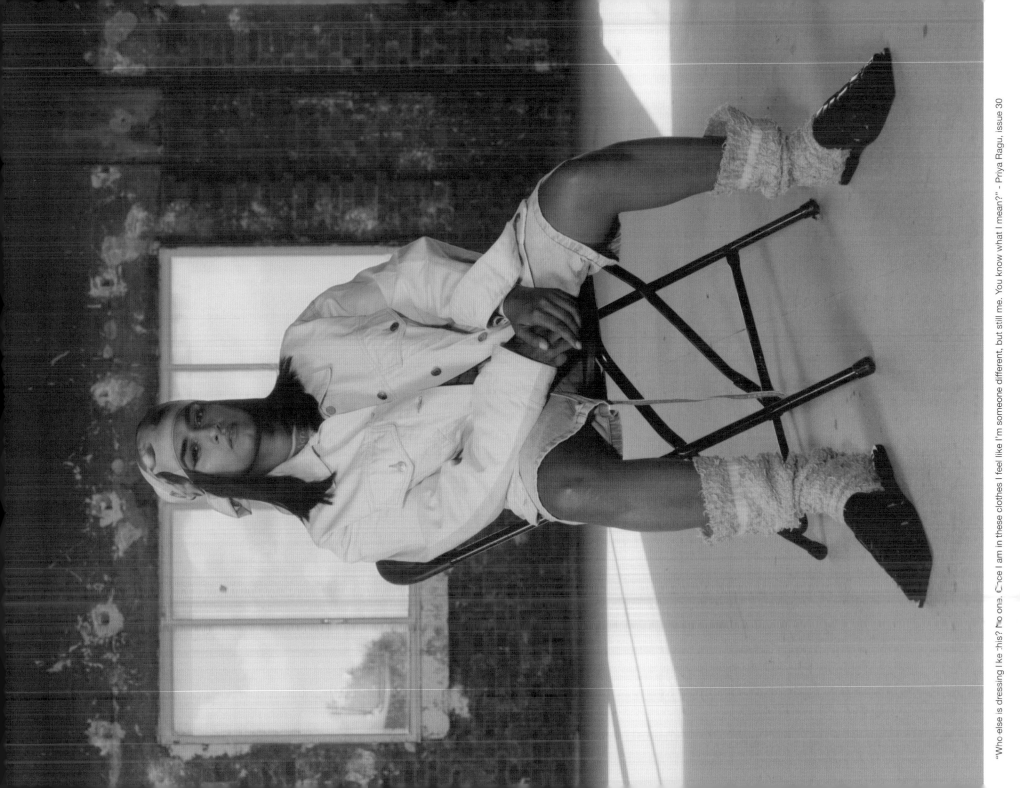

"Who else is dressing like this? No one. No one. Once I am in these clothes I feel like I'm someone different, but still me. You know what I mean?" - Priya Ragu, issue 30

Let's Eat Grandma

photographed by Clare Shilland in London

Rosa Walton: "No one is truly cool and yet at the same time everybody's cool." – Let's Eat Grandma, issue 24

GERI HALLIWELL, ISSUE 19

Were you aware at the time how difficult a girl band would be to break?

What we came up with as a band was authentic and ours, but the reason it became our sound was because we incorporated different tastes. You have this melting pot of ideas and you try and incorporate beats that one person would like and then melodies certain other people liked, so that's where you got that mish-mash of sounds. Before the Spice Girls was working as a solo artist. I'd met the other girls but we weren't a band yet and I remember thinking, "What way do I go?" I went to ask this DJ, who was quite well up the food chain, and he said, "Girl bands never work." He actually said that. But I went with what I felt. I really loved the girls and the idea of what we were doing. I always forget his name—hang on, he's an American singer-songwriter—Bob Dylan! He said, "This is not an album, this is a movement."

Is "zig-a-zig-ah" about sex?

What do you think it means?

That it's a euphemism for a shag. [Holds head in hands.]

No?

[Silence.] I think it means whatever you want it to mean.

Victoria wasn't there for the "final recording session" was she?
Who told you that?

It's on the Internet...
Oh, OK. If she's admitted that then that's fine. I think she was either shopping, or doesn't matter. Some of us... I don't know what to say. She wasn't there.

She brought other things to the band, maybe.
Yeah. That's OK. She represented something that some girls could identify with. I was fine.

But she doesn't get a line on the song, does she?
No, because she wasn't there. That's the way it rolls; if you're not there, you don't sing.

Early in your career you were often referred to as a confessional songwriter—how did you feel about that?

That's interesting... I don't see confessional as a pejorative, or something weak, but at the time I believe it was a bit misogyristic, even if a woman was saying it. I don't think people were saying the guys of my time were confessional; they were poets, they were powerful. They were revealing something to us. At that time I think confessional was a way of demeaning some of the singer-songwriters who were really trying to be dead honest. When he guys were doing it, it was like some form of high art, but when we were doing it, it was like we were reading from our diary. I did feel that sort of demeaning at the time.

This was at the time of that famous cover of Q magazine with Björk and PJ Harvey, where the headline was: "Hips. Tits. Power," which is mad to look back at now.

Yes, mad. I is mad. That's why when a journalist said the other day, "Don't you think that being a female artist now is much harder that it was in the '90s?" I said, sure, it has its challenges now. There's no question that women in music now are dealing with what they're dealing with. We didn't have social media back then, but we had magazines. We had a lot of print that doesn't exist anymore. If you had that headline now? If somebody dared to put that up next to some of the women that are part of the canon now, I don't know what would happen.

When I was a closeted teenager, I used to draw a lot of strength from your songs, especially ones that talked about finding a voice, or hard-won battles; do you think your music speaks to gay men in a specific way?

I hope so because I love them. I adore them. It's not that we don't love our liberal lesbians, we love them too, but gay men taught me how to carry myself. When I'd be having a crush on a boy at school and just going on about it, they would just be like, "OK, Tori wants, never will get! Don't you understand, that's the fastest way to turn a guy off." So they would teach me things.

I'll never forget, these gay waiters at one of the hotel bars, they just announced: "We're going to take you to the strip club." I was like 16. So I sat there drinking my Coca-Cola and they said, "You better play that piano honey or you're going to end up here."

I didn't understand bitchy queer at the time, but they didn't mean any harm. One of them was as cute as pumpkin pie while the other one—as a bit of a sadist. When he'd take off his tuxedo he would always be in leather. But he was trying to teach me through tough love, and I can see it now. He was trying to get through to my teenage self so that I didn't blow my life.

This is your last album. Why?

T-BOZ: Well, I mean we've been doing this for a long time. Things are different. The industry is different. You never know what God has planned for you later, but as of now, it's the end. You have to end somewhere at some point and retire.

CHILLI: It's been twenty-five years!

[SOLEMN SILENCE]

T-BOZ: Plus, I think it's hard to me to make timeless music, that doesn't just come out your butt like, "Whoop, I've got another 'Waterfalls' or another 'Unpretty.' Those aren't easy to come by. Timeless music is hard to come by.

After everything, what advice would you give a new generation of female musicians?

T-BOZ: I would stick to what I have always said: respect yourself. If you don't respect yourself, why should I respect you? There's a lot of stuff out now that is urging you to be a whore. I'm gonna say it the way it is—hoes are winning.

CHILLI: Hoes are winning right now. Hoes got TV shows, hoes got cheques. Hoes got commercials. It's cool to be a hoe right now. They're making it seem like hoe-ism is life!

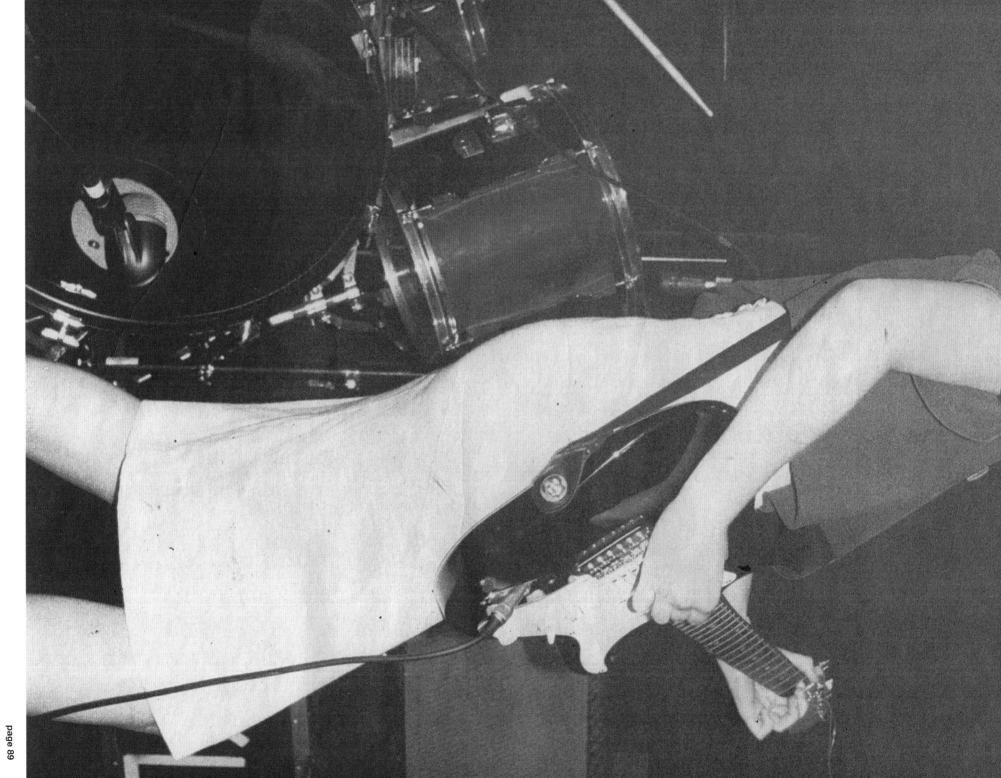

James Potter: "Life can't be perfect, it's too chaotic, but you can find beauty in it and that's as perfect as it can be." - Walt Disco, issue 31

LIZZO, ISSUE 27

How important is it for women to rely on themselves first?
I think it's important for everyone to rely or themselves
first, but I think it's important that women are taught
to rely on themselves firs because men are given that
signaling and messaging. So I feel like if we have that
message more in the media society as we have for
little boys, then I think the we wouldn't have as much
misogyny and we wouldn't put up with this bullshit as
much as we do.

"I'm not making music specifically for ony gay men." - Perfume Genius, issue 12

STORMZY, ISSUE 16

Your mum has a brilliant cameo in the "Know Me From" video. She looks like your biggest fan there, but you've said she was disappointed in you quitting your job in an oil refinery to do music.

Yeah, at first she wasn't too sure 'cause I was doing project engineering—it was a good job, the pay was alright, it was setting me up for a career for the rest of my life. Everything was going well and I decided to quit that to do music! So she was a bit confused as to why I'd throw away a prospect like that. She wasn't anti-music, she just didn't really understand. Now that it's going well... she understands.

The Eraserheads
by *Alasdair McLellan*
for issue 1
winter 2010

Diiv
by *Ryan McGinley*
for issue 6
spring 2013

Kelela
by *Lea Colombo*
for issue 23
winter 2017

The Preatures
by *Felix Cooper*
for issue 9
winter 2013

The XX
by *Alasdair McLellan*
for issue 21
spring 2017

The XX
by *Alasdair McLellan*
for issue 5
autumn 2012

Lily Allen
by *Angelo Pennetta*
for issue 10
spring 2014

Charli XCX
by *Chad Moore*
for issue 21
spring 2017

Sky Ferreira
by *Chris Stein*
for issue 15
summer 2015

Priya Ragu
by *Thomas Cristiani*
for issue 30
winter 2021

Let's Eat Grandma
by *Clare Shilland*
for issue 24
spring 2018

Pixie
by *Alasdair McLellan*
for issue 6
spring 2013

Lily Allen
by *Angelo Pennetta*
for issue 10
spring 2014

Mø
by *Clare Shilland*
for issue 19
summer 2016

Goal Girl
by *Angelo Pennetta*
for issue 20
winter 2016

Deer Spencer
by *Frank Lebon*
for issue 24
winter 2018

Walt Disco
by *Harry Freegard*
for issue 31
summer 2022

Perfume Genius
by *James Robjant*
for issue 22
winter 2017

Perfume Genius
by *Crew Jarrett*
for issue 12
autumn 2014

HC9909
by *Cameron Smith*
for issue 14
spring 2015

Jessie Ware
by *Oliver Hadlee Pearch*
for issue 13
autumn 2014

Jorja
by *Benedikt Frank*
for issue 19
summer 2016

Shy Girl
by *Liam Warwick*
for issue 28
winter 2018

Devonté Hynes
by *Crew Jarrett*
for issue
winter 2013

Bo Ningen
by *Sue Webster*
for issue 1
winter 2010

Caroline Polachek
by *Chad Moore*
for issue 10
spring 2014

Honey Hahs
by *Oliver Hadlee Pearch*
for issue 21
spring 2017

myKKi biaNCo

ISSUE 29 SUMMER 2021 FREE!

BY DANIEL JACK LYONS

interview techniques

The first person I ever interviewed invited me on tour with them to manage their merch stall. Sensing that this was a chaotic and possibly terrible idea, I turned it down. Was I right to turn down this once-in-a-lifetime opportunity? Who knows. But what I did learn that day was t'at the best way to interview someone is to be their best friend for an hour: they will spill their deepest, darkest secrets, some funny snippets about pizza, and if they shag to their own music. I don't know how many notches there are on my interview bedpost, but over time I have developed my own special technique of gently teasing the best out of people. This involves unflinchingly talking about myself first and then hoping the person I am interviewing says something like, "Oh of course, when I found out I was being cheated on, I broke into his house and spray-painted 'you arsehole' all over the kitchen!" (Although, to date, this particular story has not come up—yet). Everyone has their own way of doing things, of course. Some journalists like to do loads of research into the minutiae of their interviewees' lives, so that they know before they ask exactly why they included a marimba, or recorded the drum part on two waste bins.

Sometimes, when putting together an issue of BEAT, Michael and I like to jazz things up a bit. Perhaps we will ask an unlikely fan to interview a musician, or pull questions out of a Lady Gaga lunchbox. Once I just handed out a questionnaire, and I have also been known to do an interview that only consisted of questions that were also song titles.

People love to ask me who the best person I've interviewed has been, and then follow it up by asking who was the worst. I don't know if I can define the best and the worst, but a fairly famous pop star did burp garlic sausage in my face for an hour, and once a different musician told me that they enjoyed the risky pastime of naked falconry. I'll let you guess who you each of these were.

Why on earth did you start BEAT?
I think I wanted to edit a magazine and there wasn't one for me to edit. And I wanted to go to gigs for free.

Did you ever think of jacking it all in and living on an island?
An island where, though? Like a rock off the edge of Scotland not so much, but maybe... Jamaica?

Who would you trust to look after your dog, Beyoncé or Rihanna?
Beyoncé, one hundred per cent. Rihanna reads as a cat person.

What colour is hate?
A sort of greige, I believe.

What does love smell like?
Like a biscuit dipped in tea.

What do you look for in a person?
They have to be unafraid to wail out the chorus to 4 Non Blondes' "What's Up."

Would you ever shit on someone's doorstep?
No, but I would [redacted].

What's your favourite memory of working on BEAT?
Sitting next to you and eating cake and Maltesers and convincing everyone we were shooting Rachel Stevens.

Why journalism?
I didn't choose this life, it just chose me.

Do you think Shania Twain really meant it when she suggested she wouldn't be impressed by Brad Pitt?
Honestly, she seems so hard to please. She doesn't want Brad, a rocket scientist, a guy with a car that is well kept, or a dude that can dance. No wonder she's thumbing a lift in the middle of the desert. Being alone isn't going to keep her warm in the middle of the night, if that's what she wants!

How many "females in music" pieces have you read in your lifetime?
So many—but also, not enough.

Where is music headed next?
I really don't know! I'd like to think straight to the penthouse.

Do you think Lady Gaga still has her meat dress?
Yes, but it's a jerky jerkin now.

Is Dave Grohl really the nicest man in rock?
Is there not a nicest woman in rock category now?

Where is issue 11?
Honestly CRYPTIC!

Can you juggle?
I can multitask, if that's what you mean.

Do you believe in astrology?
I'm a woman living in 2023, it's par for the course.

What's your favourite Spice Girls song?
"If U Can't Dance" and "Mama."

Do you remember where you were when that guy from alt-J left the band?
He left?

Will BEAT ever end?
God, who knows? Maybe? It might be unstoppable, like Cher.

What do you sing in the shower?
I have quite the shower repertoire, but sadly a limited word count, so will save you from the list.

If Blondie didn't exist would you be a different person?
Yes, I'd be a brunette.

Are you still excited?
Yes! I feel so galvanised. Music's going to the penthouse, baby!

Would you ever get "Tomorrow, tomorrow, I love ya tomorrow, you're only a day away" tattooed on your leg?
Oh, you haven't seen me in shorts for a while, have you?

Is this the end?
Of questions from Lady Gaga's Lunchbox? Thankfully, yes.

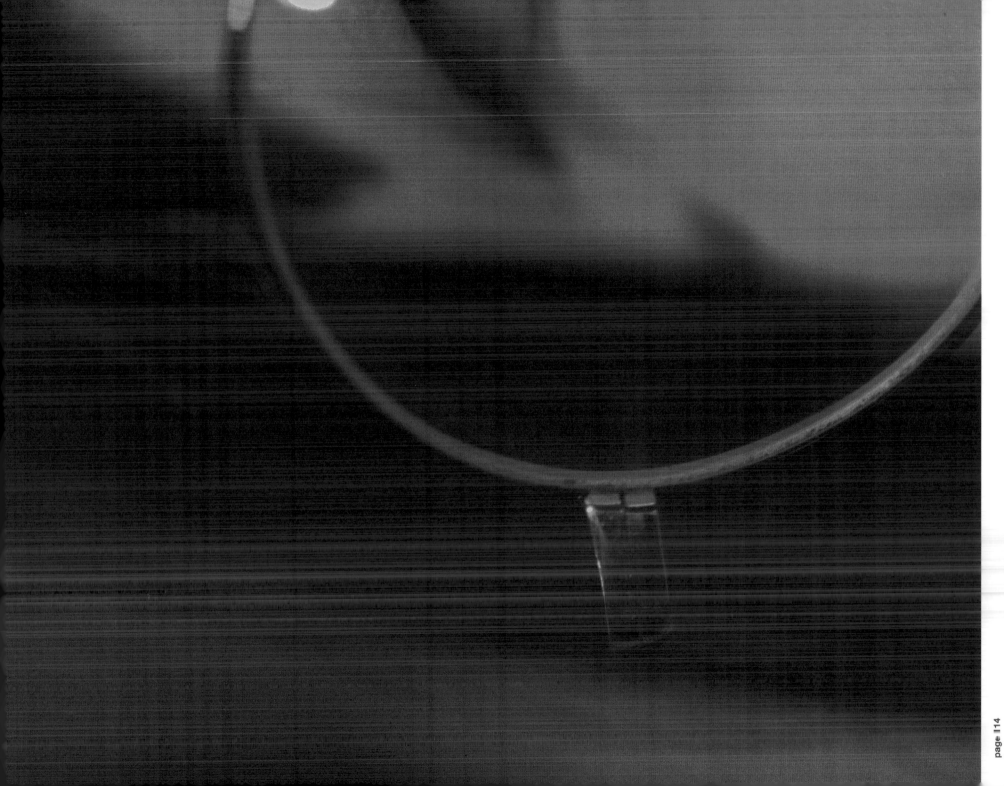

"I was an illegal immigrant; to you that's just two words, but that's a whole construct of issues followed by more issues." – BEERWYN, issue 30

Were there performers you looked to for inspiration?
Salt-N-Pepa. I was listening to early Daft Punk when it was rock. Iggy Pop, too. I loved hip-hop's directness. In no way did I think I'd be a rapper. I'm not a rapper. I speak-sing, which came from Chrissie Hynde. I loved the way she sang. Not like a Celine Dion "I'm gonna hit all these notes" way. I fucking love power ballads though. They're my fucking life.

What's your favourite?
Oh. "Total Eclipse Of The Heart." I have a whole show of power ballads. I can fucking nail them.

Considering you've had such an influence on pop music, what do you want from pop now?
It's a mess, isn't it? It's too safe. The first thing people say is that something isn't suitable for work. Who fucking cares? Go home, then.

People get scared now, too. Being scared is awesome—what do you want from music? People will come up to me after a set and say, "That was a lot of fun!" And I'm like, "Duh!"

You've been a voice for gender fluidity, sexual liberation, queerness... are you concerned it's become too topical and trendy recently?
Yeah, it's rough out there. I want trans rights to be seen for what they really mean—proper healthcare. I don't want it to just be the basis for another reality show. You want new languages and new systems, and that doesn't happen overnight. I try very hard and I always have to be sensitive.

What does it mean to be punk now?
Just to fucking do your shit. It's not about having a bad attitude. Do what you feel you really need to do, not the shit other people are doing.

BEAT

Issue 2 - Spring 17
Bones, Haha...ittle Simz, Olly Alexander
The xx/Charli XCX, Blondie

Free! thebeatjuice.com

The Rebel
Little Simz

photographed
by Will Robson-Scott

Dream Wife

Photographed by Meg Lavender

"It's also good to say at shows "You are my bad bitches — if anyone's being terrible to you, sexist or showing you aggression, let me know and I will kick them out." It's as simple as that." — Rakel, Dream Wife

atmosphere of the room. It's also good to say at shows "You are my bad bitches — if anyone's being terrible to you, sexist or showing you aggression, let me know and I will kick them out." It's as simple as that. Everyone should have the right to feel safe at a gig and have fun.

You posted the lyrics to Somebody as a response to #metoo. Do you think artists with a platform almost have a duty to use it to comment on major issues like that?
We're still a young band but the more it does grow, that's when you become more aware. Around the time of #metoo we got four different messages from people tattooing the lyrics "I am not my body I am somebody"

Wait, is it made of real snails or is that just a name?
The snails don't get hurt! They go to a spa and that's how they make all the snail juice because they feel comfortable, and all the liquid from that juice is mixed together with some stuff and then you put it on your face.

Wow, that sounds disgusting. How often do you check your horoscope?
Every month — me and Alice are both Sagittarius and Bella's a Leo. Usually our horoscopes are spot on. I like to read it at the beginning of the month and again at the end. Then I'm like, that was so true. How did she know??

You sing a bit of Wannabe during F.U.U. Do you think Dream Wife would exist if the Spice Girls hadn't?
I don't know. Spice Girls had a huge influence on our childhoods. To say whatever you want to say and not to have to be perfect as women and especially girls are told to be at such a young age. We actually had to get clearance to use that line [from Wannabe] — we didn't get it in time so it's only a live version now. We hand-wrote a letter to the Spice Girls.

"Sometimes there will be lines that I laugh at when thinking about anyone else hearing them." - Gracie Abrams, issue 30

"Everything is just so fucked and difficult. But I think it's picking and choosing and prioritising the battles that you want to fight for." – Kelsey Lu, issue 25

"I remember seeing Peaches play a lot ages ago and her backup dancers had strap-ons and there was a lot of... making them helicopter." - St. Vincent, issue 26

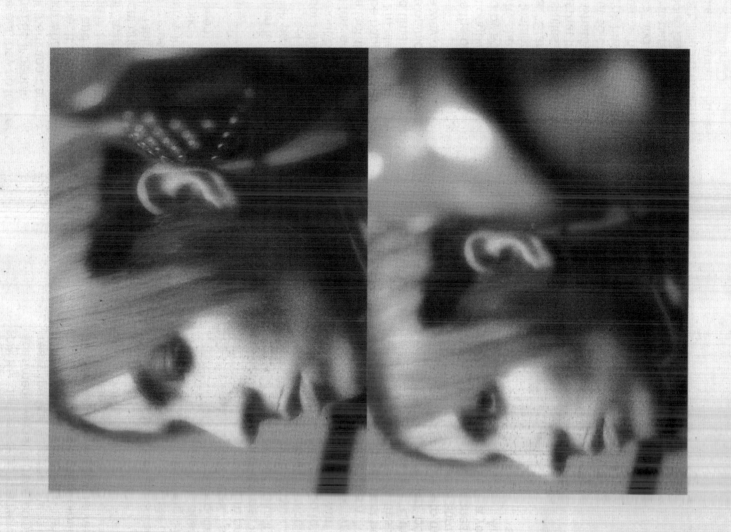

mix

limited edition

by [?] linskell

ISSUE 31 SUMMER 2022 FREE!

MUNA & CLARA BALZARY

HAVE I GOT
YOUR ATTENTION

Dua

FREE!

BEAT

we will always be together in electric dreams   giorgio moroder

what is good taste anyway?

It is theorised that Paleolithic cave paintings in several different caves around the world served more than one purpose. Some of them act as a calendar, marking where the moon is in relation to various beasts' mating and birthing seasons, and some of them are painted in "points of resonance," which basically means that if you stood at the mouth of the cave and banged a drum or clapped your hands, by the time the sound bounced all the way down the cave, it would be reverb-ing and echoing like crazy and you'd go into what scientists have referred to as "an awe-inspired state."

These Stone Age soundtracks appear elsewhere, in burial mounds that have a certain rhythmic frequency. Research has been done to show that drumming at the same frequency (obviously you can't get inside the mound) results in an elevated pulse rate and heightened breathing. Sound familiar?

We can't hop in a time machine and go back and check out these early cave raves, but my point is that music has been twisting people's melons for at least 13,000 years, if not more. The day the first goat hide was stretched over a dried-out gourd to make a drum and Stone Age man banged out a rhythm was also the day that music taste was born.

I don't believe in good taste or bad taste; it's an oxymoron to me, like saying something is awfully good, or definitely maybe. I like all sorts of music, some sorts more than others, admittedly, but I am always willing to give something a try for at least thirty seconds—or even up to the chorus and beyond, just in case it's really great. Or I might listen to something once, then come back to it later on. There are some bands that I just wasn't into until I'd had my heart broken for the first time, because I had no idea of how that particular sadness sounded, and what I was listening to before that just didn't make sense.

So taste really is whatever you decide you like, for no other reason than you like it. Some people try to define taste as something you were born with, or something you can cultivate. People who think that they alone have good taste, I find, tend to be quite bossy. The dictionary defines taste as "the ability to recognise beauty in something." Did I recognise beauty in wearing jeans so tight I could barely breathe, with five-pound plimsolls, and listening to the Klaxons? At the time I thought I was the height of sophistication and, well, retrospectively (and sorry to any Klaxon reading this)—not so much. It goes without saying that a lot of what is deemed good taste is funnelled to us by obsessive freaks who just love music so much that they have to make a magazine about it—or DJs, or journalists, or the radio. This is, ahem, honed by marketing budgets and influenced by those who wield power, such as friends who we think have good taste, or people who are just loud about what they like. Then there are other deciding factors, like how many followers someone has, or whether they are followed by a Kardashian. Does having a million followers on Instagram make someone more enjoyable to listen to than someone who doesn't?

In the philosopher Pierre Bourdieu's book *Distinction: A Social Critique of the Judgement of Taste*, he notes that good taste was really just a way of society's ruling class to separate themselves from the poor and less powerful. Perhaps this is why having a love for cheesy pop music is described as a guilty pleasure, or people think that they've reached enlightenment if they love Nick Drake. Well, I have something to admit: I love pop music, and if Nick Drake comes on the stereo I have to switch it off. Sorry Nick, but you just don't give me an elevated pulse rate in the same way that a good old-fashioned pop banger does.

Some of my favourite musical moments have included driving across Los Angeles at night, listening to Phil Collins at full volume as the world wobbles past the window. Or the time I saw Siouxsie Sioux play and I was sitting next to PJ Harvey, and she made notes in a wee notepad she fished out of her handbag. Or the time I DJed and played this stomping remix of *A Fifth of Beethoven* (which in itself is a funky remix of Beethoven's Fifth Symphony, by Walter Murphy and his band) and was totally unprepared for how wild everyone would go. Or the time I saw Fleet Foxes in the desert and it was magical, even though I didn't know any of their songs and historically had thought I wasn't really into "that" sort of music.

Whether or not I like it, taste does define our lives. It informs where we live and how we live and what we put in our bodies, what we watch on the TV, how we relax. If we were dating and you rocked up in a Lighthouse Family T-shirt and started reciting the lyrics to "Ocean Drive," it's likely you might find yourself quickly single again. But taste is chaotic. It knows no boundaries. You can love Mariah Carey and The Make Up. You can sing along to Sinéad O'Connor and Little Mix, and the truth is that maybe we should be a little more open to trying both ends of the spectrum. If you're a pop purist, maybe give some groovy funk a go? If you consider anything without a guitar unworthy of your ears, get some deep-cut disco on your headphones. There is so much pleasure that has been derived in such a broad scope of music. Taste has nothing to do with it. Taste exists without rules, it can't be borrowed or taught, it just comes from inside.

Brian D'Addario: "Most indie bands, they put most effort into the style and presentation of their ideas. Making sure it coincides with something that feels cool. But when you break it d

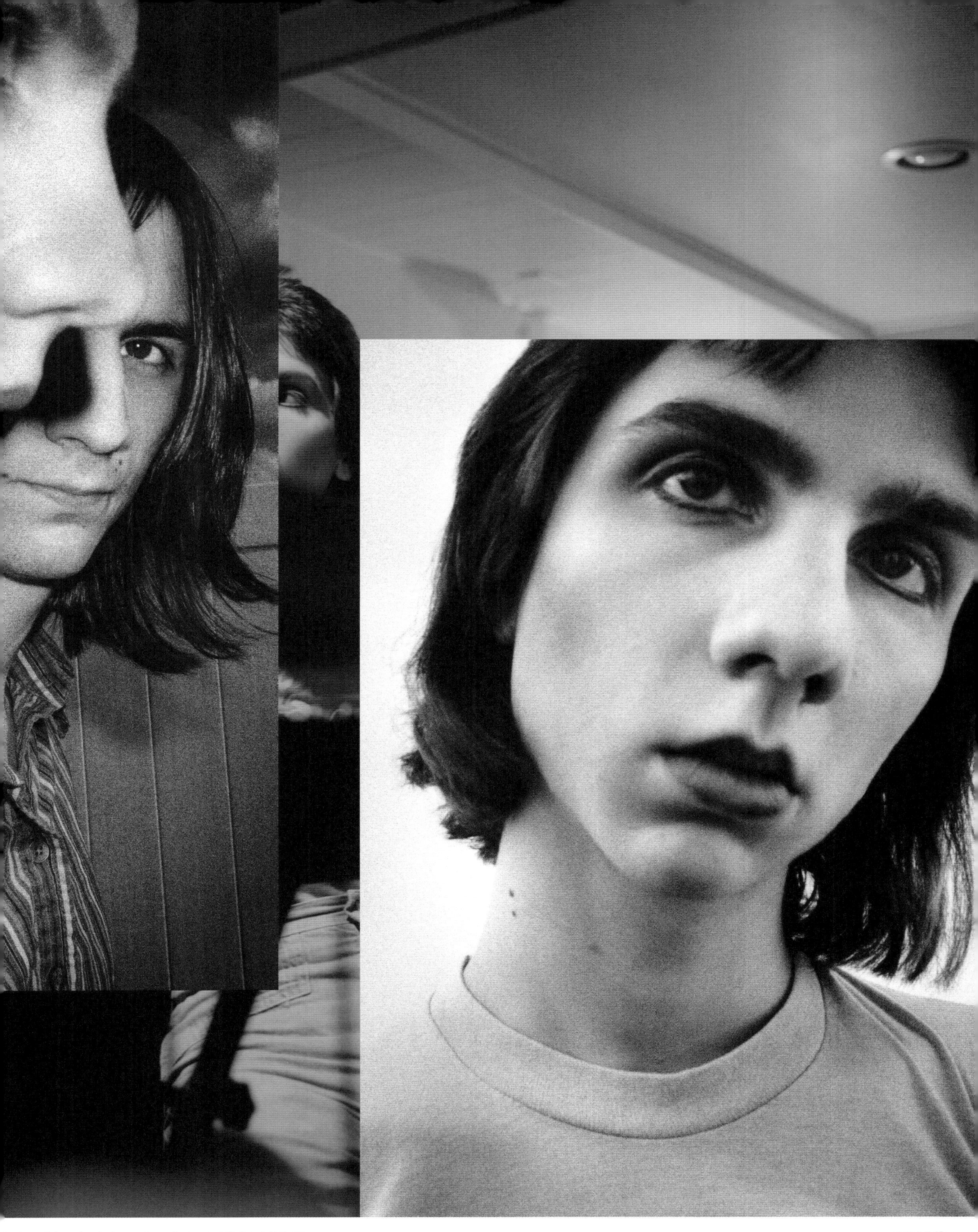

ere's nothing of substance there." - Lemon Twigs, issue 19

NICK CAVE, JIM SCLAVUNOS, AND WARREN ELLIS, ISSUE 1

"It's so physical," states Nick. "If you can get to that place where you're abandoned - it's great. But if you don't get there, then it's a nightmare."

There are moments on stage where you are really connecting and you feel it. And sometimes you don't. It's not like something you can chase, it's just something that just sort of happens."

Jim Sclavunos agrees: "Ideally you get that unself-consciousness that you do when you're in the middle of a nice improv, where you're just making music and not really evaluating, measuring or judging yourself. When the audience gets into the same space, it's amazing. You can feel everything change for them. It's always a good sign when you leave a gig and you stand outside the venue and you think, 'Holy shit, how did I get here?' There's a cause, we all look at each other. Nick breaks it. "If you're connecting with the band, if you're in the same mental space, then it works. You can be a fifteen-stone midget and still wanna be on stage, that's what rock and roll is."

"My awakening to the gift of music was ey iude" - Desire Marea, issue 30

GIORGIO MORODER, ISSUE 14

*Did you ever "feel love" while listening to that song—i.e.,
did you ever use your own music to soundtrack sweet
lovemaking?*

For late at night? Hmm, no. That would distract me
(laughs). I would think, "Oh, who played bass on this?
Which studio was this recorded in?"

You'd need to focus.
  Right.

*I've got to ask about your 1985 album That's
Bubblegum—That's Giorgio. And was the meaning
behind the title?*

  I don't know. I can't ever know what you're talking
about. What was the title?

That's Bubblegum—That's Giorgio.
  Oh. Probably because I love bubblegum. Oh dear.

You had another album called Solitaire . . .
  That was a disaster.

*. . . the cover of which features you saddled a naked
lady literally covered in spinach.*
  That was the idea.

beat page fifty three

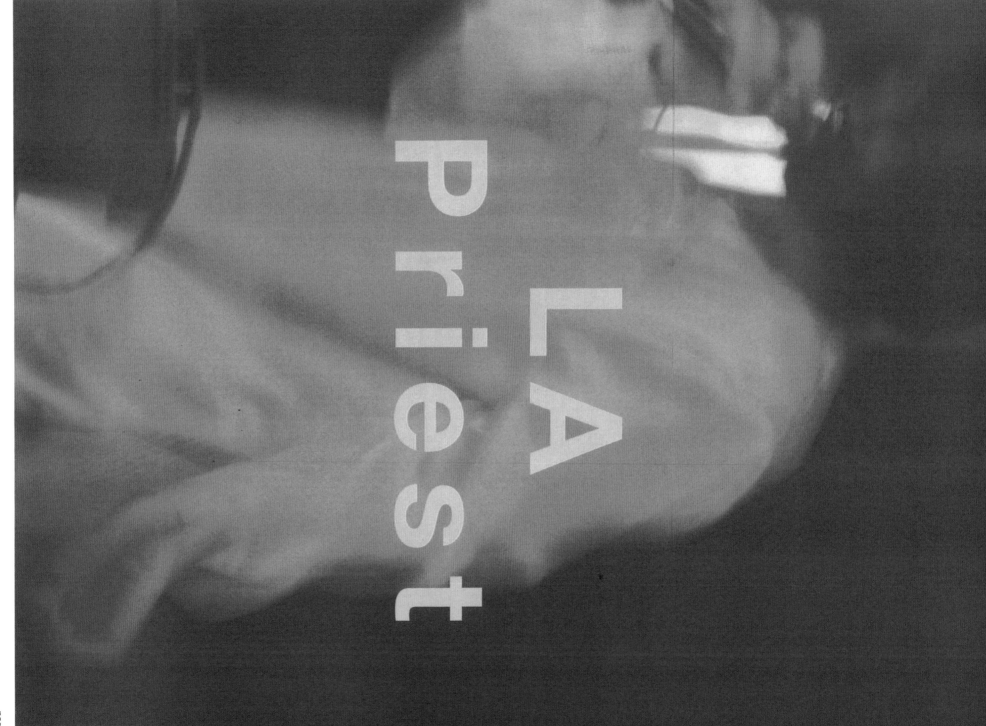

LA Priest

"I just want to do it all. I want to be able to make being a mother work with being a singer." - Jessie Ware, issue 12

BLONDIE, ISSUE 11

What's your life philosophy?
DEBBIE HARRY: Oh God! I guess I beat myself up and say, "Eugh, you're not this and you're not that, but my God, you've had this incredible, explanatory life."
CHRIS STEIN: Maybe that's the secret, not thinking how great you are.
DEBBIE: I don't think I'm really I usually think I'm a complete schmuck. I think I'm an achiever type, I always want to do things better. It's not to gain things. It's to do better.

Do you live in the moment?

CHRIS: That's a great question. People ask us all the time, "Did you think you'd be doing this for forty years?" and the answer is...

DEBBIE: FUCK NO!

CHRIS: The answer is that I've evolved very much in the moment certainly back then and now. I don't want to think about...
DEBBIE: You don't want to think about walking through airports with luggage? I don't know what's wrong with you?
You carry your own luggage
DEBBIE: I can't stand it. I have my favourite pair of shoes to someone and then a sneaker.
CHRIS: I keep telling her, Blondie does not carry her own luggage.
DEBBIE: She has multiple pairs of shoes.
So, really, we could make you better with more shoes.
DEBBIE: Yes, that's it! More shoes.

"I pioneered the path for Lil Nas X to come up, so the idea that I would ever in any way be pitted against literally my daughter is bizarre." - Mykki Blanco, issue 29

"I'm desperate for connection, but I observe things trough a lens. I'm extremely interested in cocumentation." - Okay Kaya, issue 32

Laura Les: "Did you know that everything is in retrograde right now? There's six planets in retrograde or something. I don't know what that means, but I do know that shit's crazy." – 100

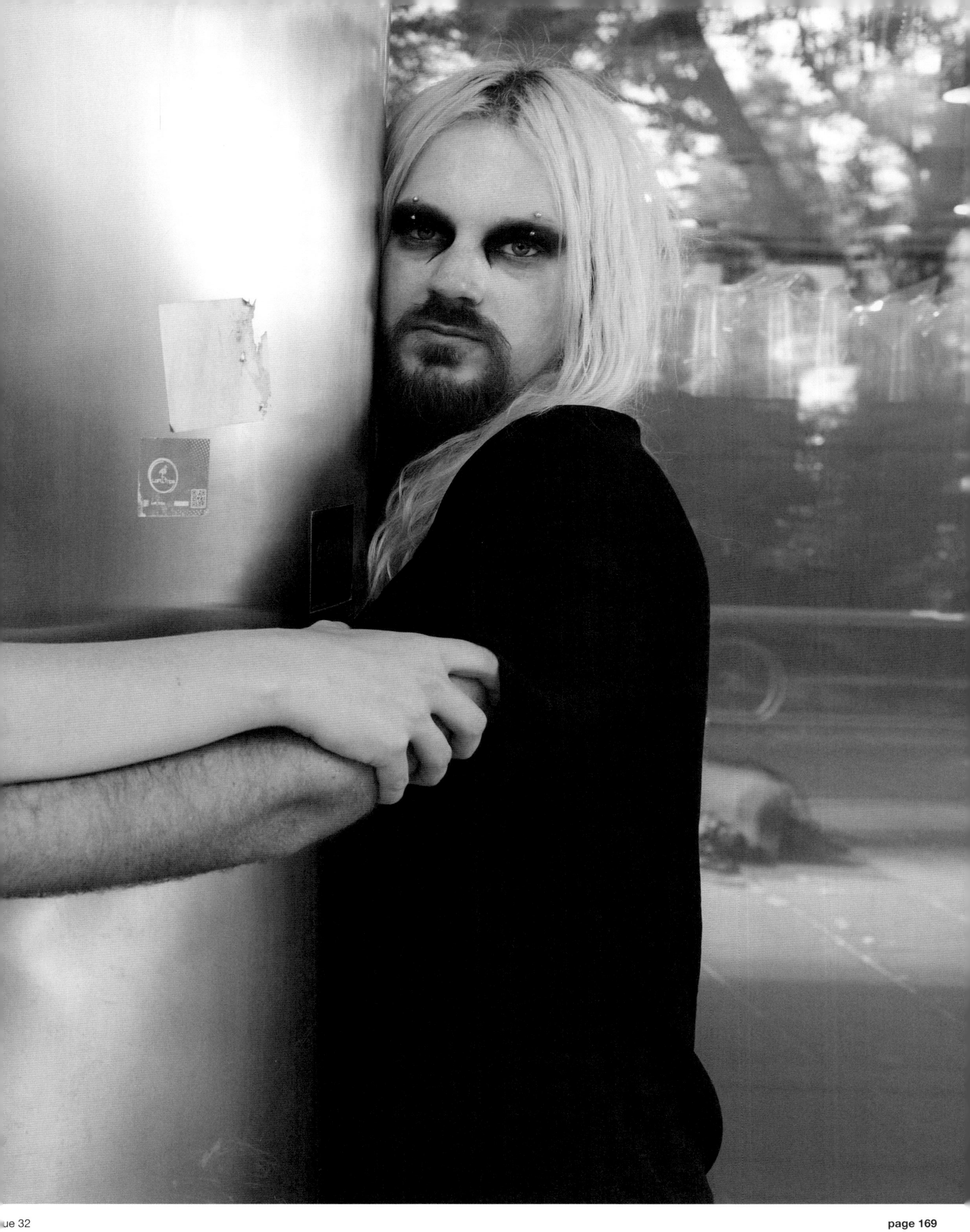

Dua Lipa
by Harina Moon
for issue 28
autumn winter 2018

Little Mix
by Ian McKell
for issue 15
winter 2015

Giorgio Moroder
by Max Farago
for issue 14
spring 2014

Muna
by Clara Balzary
for issue 31
summer 2022

Sigrid
by Clare Shilland
for issue 23
spring 2017

Chilli and Marley
by Benedikt Frank
for issue 22
winter 2016

Leeron Twigs
by Andreas Laszlo Konrath
for issue 19
summer 2016

Tink
by Chad Moore
for issue 5
winter 2015

Desire Marea
by Jamal Nxedlana
for issue 30
winter 2021

Georgia
by Letty Schmiterlov
for issue 24
winter 2017

Wu Lyf
by Michael Hautpman
for issue 3
winter 2011

Yeasayer
by Drew Jarrett
for issue 18
winter 2019

Flohio
by William Spooner
for issue 31
winter 2022

A Friest
by Jonathan Vincent Baron
for issue 15
winter 2015

Jessie Ware
by Clare Shilland
for issue 23
spring 2017

Courtney Barnett
by Pooneh Ghana
for issue 30
winter 2021

Maui Phoenix
by Lewis Vorn
for issue 31
spring 2022

Mykki Blanco
by Daniel Jack Lyons
for issue 29
summer 2021

Empress Of
by Chad Moore
for issue 16
winter 2015

Okay Kaya
by Rumi Bauermann
for issue 32
winter 2022

100 Gecs
by Dexter Lander
for issue 32
winter 2022

These New Puritans
by Angelo Pennetta
for issue 27
summer 2017

Bree Runway
by Felix Cooper
for issue 29
summer 2021

five years, what a surprise

The text arrived from Carl, arguably one of the most important people in music, the gatekeeper to many of the world's biggest pop stars, on a Saturday afternoon. I was in the garden centre looking at plant pots. It simply said: "Do you want to shoot Miss Beyoncé?" I twirled round in the aisle next to the big bags of compost. DID I? I DID I WANT TO SHOOT BEYONCÉ? "Of course!" I replied nonchalantly.

Contracts were signed. Codenames were employed. Budget was begged, borrowed, and a tiny bit stolen. I had produced BEAT for exactly five years, we'd created 14 issues, and I tried not to give away the fact that I felt wildly out of my depth, waking up in the middle of the night on L.A. time to sign contracts and go over how many motor homes we needed and what was on the rider. I faked it until I really did make it from my little basement in Dalston. I couldn't mention any of this to anyone in case it suddenly became not real—but also because I was contractually obliged not to.

The day I sent the issue with Beyoncé to the printers and tried to imagine what would happen next, an email slid into view. It was from a publicist called Julian. Julian looked after lots of bands, and David Bowie. Years ago I wrote him a letter saying that I would love to do David Bowie. I kissed the envelope as I put it in the post box and never heard back from either Julian or David.

Can you give me a call? Wanna chat to you about something.

I replied, sassy and confident, buoyed by Beyoncé.

Of course, I'd love to have David Bowie as my next cover after Beyoncé xo

Two days later and the Beyoncé cover is everywhere. It's on her Instagram and mine, and everyone else's

in between. The Times of India are calling me and The New York Times and The Guardian. The whole world is surprised that Beyoncé has graced the cover of a small, independently published magazine, and when Julian calls me, before I can say hello, he says:

"I thought you were joking about Beyoncé." I smile and say no. I wasn't! He says, "Well I wanted to talk to you because David's seen the BEAT and he wants to do something." And suddenly I can't breathe. There's a pause. Julian continues, "What do you think?"

I'm taking the call outside an ice cream shop in Dalston. It's a stinky hot day. Tears spring out of my eyes. I put the phone down to Julian and take six quick breaths then call him back. What I think is YES.

I have loved, in the purest sense of the word, David Bowie since I first saw him as Jareth, the Goblin King. I spent a year of my life listening to The Rise and Fall of Ziggy Stardust (both sides) on vinyl, twice, before I left the house every day. I have seen all of his films. I have been to Berlin. I even know that his mum handed Siouxsie Sioux a copy of "The Laughing Gnome" on 7-inch in the street, when she was just a teenager in Bromley, where he grew up. I've had a framed picture of him from 1981 on my wall since I was a student, and when I listen to him I feel like I am nothing more than matter floating in space. I suppose that's what he was aiming for all these years.

David won't do anything for us, other than pick out his favourite pictures, and that is fine, it's perfect. What else could you ask for?

We decide to print the issue as big as we can, four times the normal size. When you go to the printers

it's like magic, the paper starts off on a giant roll and whirs and spins and the images appear and disappear and then the issue appears, hanging above your head. Then it travels around the room so the ink can dry, before being delivered onto a conveyor belt and put into a bundle. There is a little hatch in one of the machines and if you open it, it delivers you a perfect—or perhaps imperfect—issue, hot, literally, off the press.

So this issue will be special. It will be huge, and for the cover we will make a collage out of pictures of David from different eras. I love it so much. It's so perfect. I send it to Julian for David to check.

I imagine David unfolding the giant pages of my magazine in his apartment in New York, unfolding each page and smoothing it out with the back of his hand. I like to cut things fine, so the day before the magazine goes to print I start to write an editor's letter, but I don't really know what to say. What do you say? So I close the laptop and go to bed. When I wake up, everything has changed.

I text Julian to ask if I am awake and this is real. He calls me back. I stand and look out of the window, people on the street carry on with life, and think about David Bowie. Julian told me that he'd sent David the cover to see. To make sure that he liked it. This image, a little collage of a man that meant so much to me, made of scraps of pictures. He'd replied to Julian.

I love it, DB.

Debbie Harry: "Punk, really, was an idea. It wasn't about a particular style of music. We come from the beginnings of it, which was more about a certain attitude, a change in the status

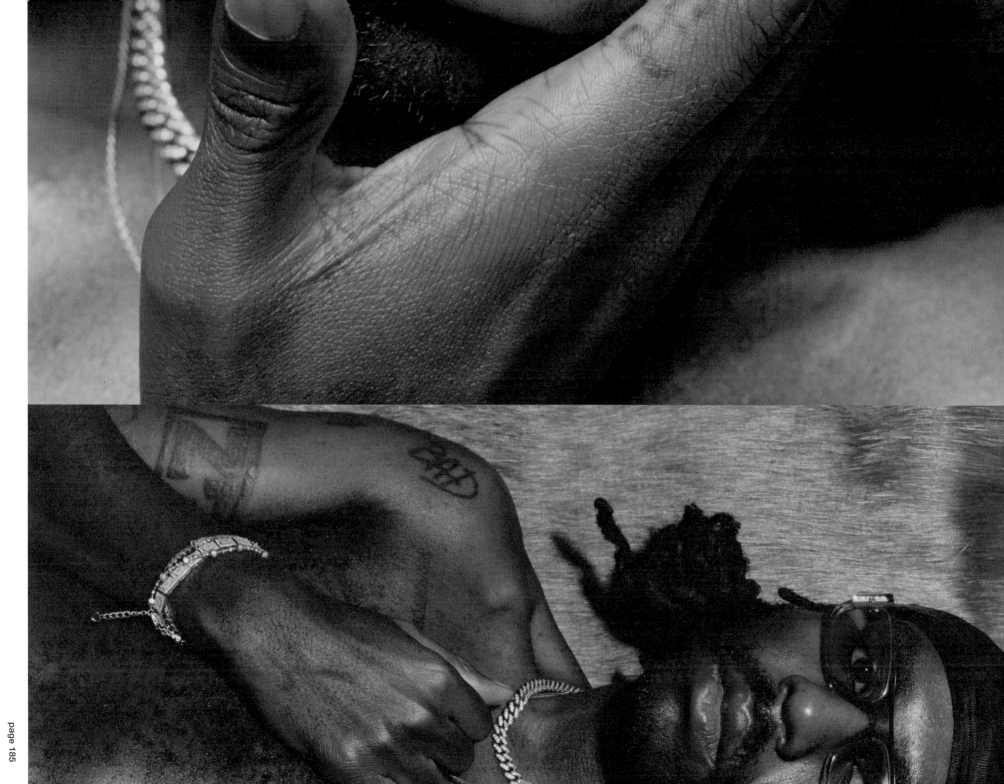

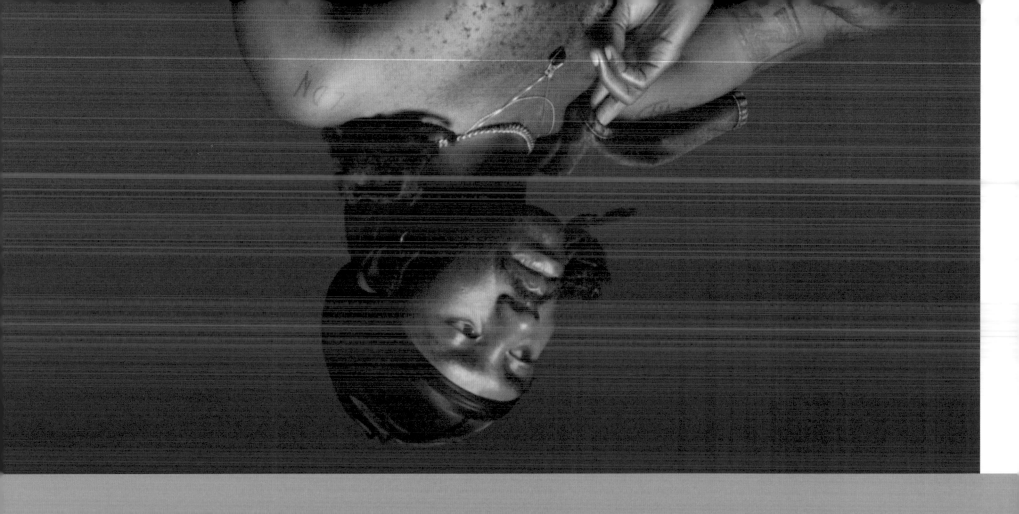

DEVONTE HYNES, ISSUE 25

Speaking of luxury, I love that Fet Daddy is on the album – how did that happen?

[Laughs] Yeah, that was a wild one. Basically, we had gotten to be friends since the last album came out. It's weird, we somehow got holdof it and then was doing Snap chat stories with my reward in the background! Anyway, someone then gave him m number ard we started hanging out a lot and talking a lot.

Was there a specific thought process behind what collaborators you got involved in the album?

There's actually zero thought process—which is crazy. I rarely reach out to artists. And it's strange to do with ego—it's the exact opposite—is that I'm not worthy to reach out to artists, and the prospect of doing it terrifies me.

Surely at this point you must be more confident?

I'm still just really scared. I'm confident to the point where I know what I can do for myself, but outside of that the confidence stops.

Hello, Genesis.

Hi, sorry, I've just slept over. I set the alarm and then slept through it. I was having this weird dream. I'd taken over this old strip club, right. There were these people trying to convince me they had this great new act, riding bicycles round and round in circles. Were they all naked? Oh God, I wish. No, I'm just going to make a cup of tea. Can you call back in ten minutes?

Just out of interest, Genesis, how do you take your tea?

As hot as I can stand it, with honey, milk, and Twinings Breakfast Tea. The amber of the Queen's England, as Quentin Crisp used to say.

How much love goes into what you do?

Look, you wouldn't decide to dedicate your life to attacking the status quo and the bigots and hypocrites in power unless you love both humanity and other people, beyond the fear of being destroyed. You have to love so much that you could be destroyed, even killed for what you believe. That's an incredible amount of love. Happiness is always connected with being loved, for me. You know, the untrammelled, unselfconscious happiness comes from knowing that somebody—a friend, a lover, a somebody—loves and adores me for myself. Everything else, what I've done, what I've not done, what I'm trying to achieve, all of that becomes irrelevant when I realise that they just adore and love me, little Gen.

"You know when people say things like 'Ooh, look up to the moon, we're all under the same moon?' I feel like it's from *Armageddon*, even if I prefer *Deep Impact*. Anyway, that's what I

-formed idea of shared consciousness." - Olly Alexander, issue 21

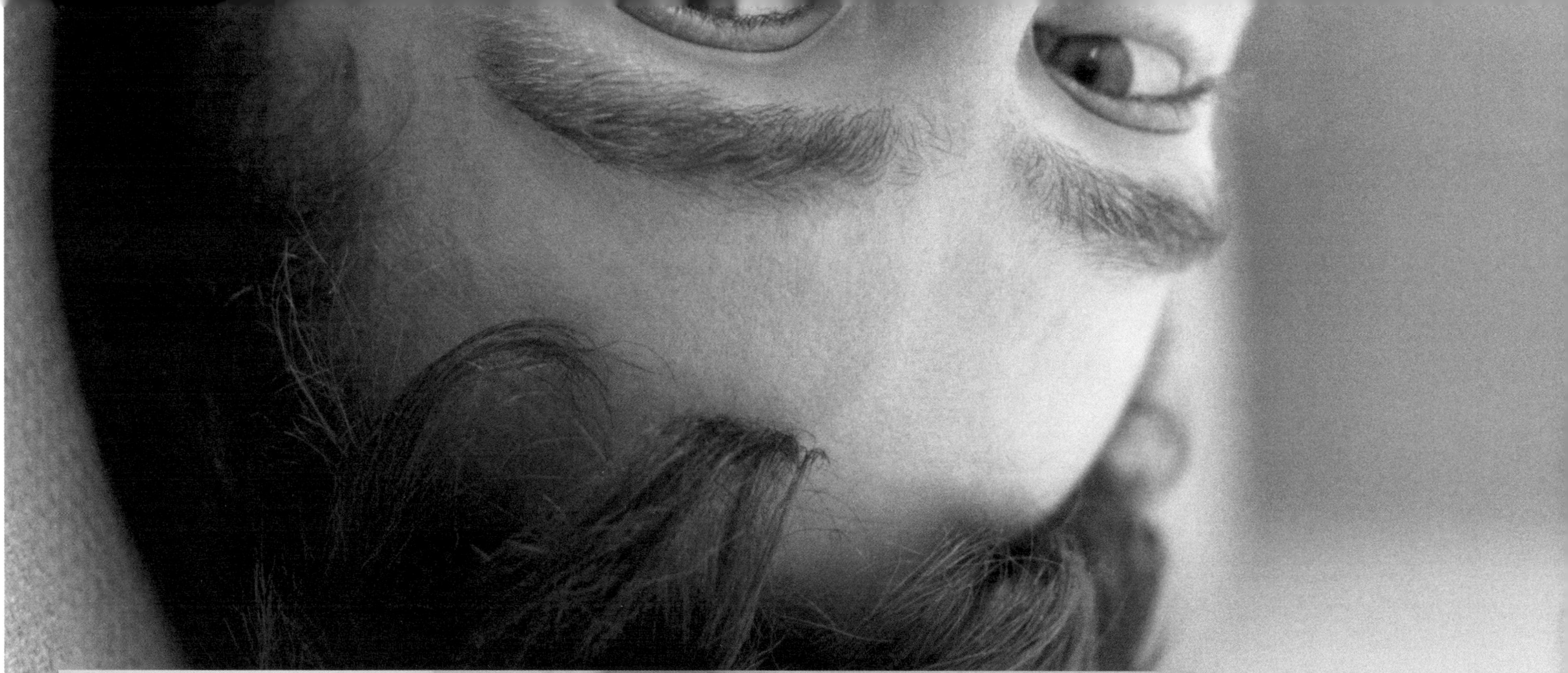

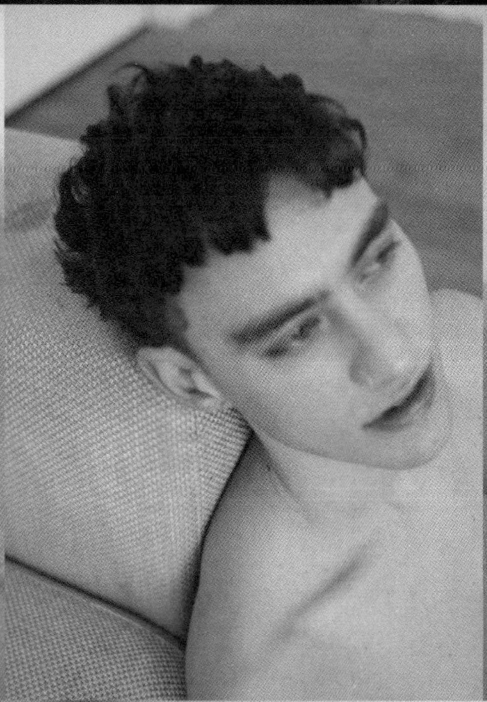

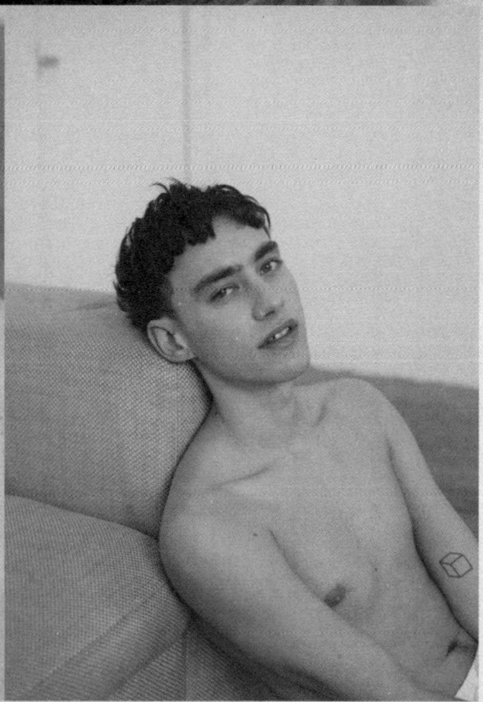

CAT POWER, ISSUE 26

In 2013 I got in the car at the airport with an old lover from Atlanta, and the song [that is "Say"] was on the radio... got in the car and he said, "There's my girl," I thought he was talking about me but he was talking about her so I got a bit little thing and he turned the radio off a few years after that, I was in a cab and for, like, fifteen blocks all the way the cathartic was... "All about it was a fever." I love Rihanna's connection with people but I had never really engage... in the holy power... and she felt; her vibrating resonance. I was like she was sitting in the car with me, lamenting

When a singer is able to let your pain live, it helps you feel like there's empathy on the earth. The words are just a translation,

but it's the sound of her voice. Listener heard Aretha Franklin sing "Amazing Grace," I cried, because I had been taught horrible things about God but when I hear her sing I understood what the holy spirit was. It's like hearing magic. It allows you - draws, it opens your ear. You get recharged, your can reel your life.

In the olden days of music, - e 50s and 60s and 70s, everyone played each others music traditionals, tribals folk singers, jazz musicians, blues musicians, classical musicians. Leonard Cohen covered Nina Simone, David Bowie covered Leonard Cohen. I covered Rihanna, but someone else will do it too. It's the same song, but that song touches the human being - is singing it, so it will always be different. Someone else will cover the song, and that's how it is. You have to think of the highest vibration of love.

If you could sign one other girl band member on loan, past or present, who would you pick?

LEIGH-ANNE: Oh my God. Beyoncé, right?

JESY: I don't know, she'd set all the limelight. I'm not sure about that. Maybe one of the Spice Girls.

PERRIE: Geri!

LEIGH-ANNE: Mine would be Mel B. "We absolutely love Sporty Spice and Baby Spice, we've met them loads of times and they're so lovely. I still call them by those nicknames, actually. Imagine us doing a collab with the Spice Girls!

JADE: In this day and age!"

LEIGH-ANNE: Yes.

JADE: Why aye.

PERRIE: I wouldn't be able — get on the vocals! I'd be dead on the floor. Mel C was in our "Word Up" video and that was enough drama for me for one day. I can't breathe when I'm around him, it's weird. They're incredible.

LEIGH-ANNE: Didn't you meet Victoria Beckham?

PERRIE: I didn't speak to them but I saw them at the closing ceremony at the Olympics and they were just walking down the corridor and I felt like I was watching the movie because they were all holding hands. Geri's so crazy in real life. She told me she loved Little Mix and what we were about and I had a tear in my eye.

How would her friends describe her? "Probably quite blunt and to-the-point," she says, er, bluntly. "I'm probably the most honest, in-your-face person... like, if a mate said, 'What do you think of this dress?' I would never be the person to lie to them. Or scheme with boys. "Complete wrong 'un, get rid of them." She laughs. There must be so much flakery in this industry, how girl? "Either I invoke a 'be kind' policy, or say things to my face," she shrugs. "Just be honest. I don't need yes people."

"I actually tried some 'shrooms the other day and I had a reflective moment of like 'wow.' Not even achievements, it was like, 'I have a fucking car and I have a house and I have fans a um.' I usually don't do that, I guess, because I'm very much an 'OK, let's keep moving' person." – Lil Nas X, issue 30

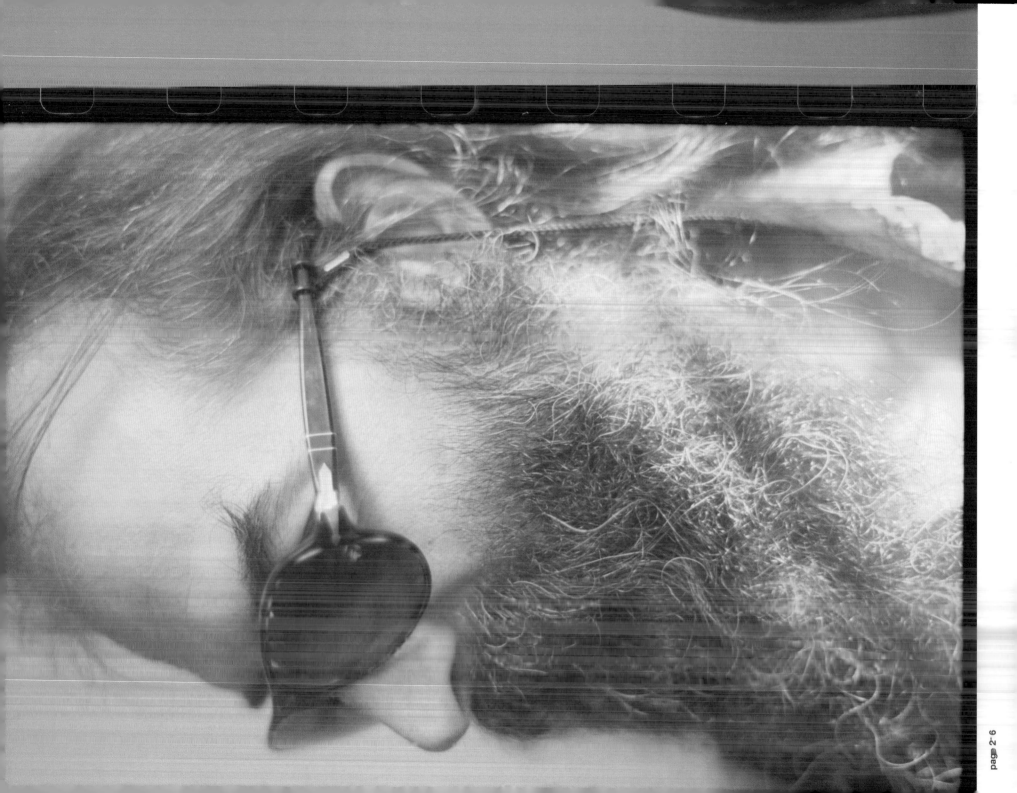

Neneh Cherry
by *Clare Shilland*
for issue 25
spring 2018

Lil Nas X
by *Felix Cooper*
for issue 30
winter 2021

Bobby Gillespie
by *Angelo Pennetta*
for issue 18
spring 2016

Giorgio Moroder
by *Max Farago*
for issue 14
spring 2014

Rina Sawayama
by *Jack Davison*
for issue 16
spring 2015

Warren Ellis and Nick Cave
by *Tyrone Lebon*
for issue 1
winter 2010

David Bowie collage
by *Jack Walsh*
for issue 17
spring 2016

Blondie
by *Andreas Lazlo Conrath*
for issue 21
summer 2017

Oliver Sims
by *Laura Jane Coulson*
for issue 31
spring 2022

Devonté Hynes
by *Oliver Hadlee Pearch*
for issue 25
summer 2018

Genesis P-Orridge
by *Hugo Scott*
for issue 26
winter 2018

Olly Alexander
by *Clare Shilland*
for issue 21
summer 2017

Cat Power
by *Clare Shilland*
for issue 26
winter 2018

Kamasi Washington
by *Jamie Hawkesworth*
for issue 23
winter 2013

Stormzy
by *Will Robson Scott*
for issue 16
winter 2015

King Princess
by *Chad Moore*
for issue 27
spring 2019

Little Mix
by *Ian McKell*
for issue 15
spring 2015

Dua Lipa
by *Hanna Moon*
for issue 29
winter 2019

thank you to all of the contributors, writers, photographers and musicians who continue to contribute their time to BEAT.

Alasdair McLellan, Alice Dellal, Alisa Smirnova, Andrea Bjorksdottir, Andreas Lazlo Konrath, Angelo Pennetta, Anna Meacham, Benedikt Frank, Bolade Banjo, Cameron Smith, Camille, Summers-Valli, Clara Balzary, Carl Fysh, Chad Moore, Chris Cuff, Chris Stein, Clare Shilland, Daniel Jack Lyons, Dexter Lander, Drew Jarret, Errol Rainey, Felix Ccoper, Frank Lebon, Grace Difford, Hanna Moon, Harry Freegard, Hobbes Ginsberg, Hugo Scott, Ian McKell, Ivan Ruberto, Jack Davison, James Robjant, Jamie Hawksworth, Jeannette Lee, Jeff Henrikson, Jon Wilkinson, Jonathan Vincent Baron, Keong Woo, Laura Coulson, Lea Colombo, Letty Schmiterlow, Lewis Vorn, Liam Warwick, Max Farago, Meg Lavender, Michael Hauptman, Murray Chalmers, Noam Klar, Oliver Hadlee Perch, Poonia Ghana, Rafael Rios, Rob Chute, Rumi Baumann, Ryan McGinley, Seb Burford, Thomas Christiani, Tyrone Lebon, Vincent Haycock, Will Robson Scott, and William Spooner.

Extra thank yous to Dean Langley, Jonny Lu, Paul Flynn, Russell Stone, Michael Cragg, Lizzie Sims, Avigail Collins, Damian Collins, Owen Meyers, Sabrina Scott, Shirley Manson, Sue Webster, and Caroline and Pippa Ratky.

First published in the United States of America in 2023 by
Rizzoli International Publications, Inc.
300 Park Avenue South, New York, NY 10010
www.rizzoliusa.com

Copyright © 2023 Hanne Hanna

Publisher: Charles Miers
Editor: Jacob Lehman
Production Manager: Kaija Markoe
Production Assistant: Olivia Fussair
Managing Editor: Lynn Scrabis

Design by Sabrina Scott

Printed in China

2023 2024 2025 2026 / 10 9 8 7 6 5 4 3 2 1
ISBN: 978-0-8478-9922-7
Library of Congress Control Number: 2023935436

Facebook.com/RizzoliNewYork
Twitter: @Rizzoli_Books
Instagram.com/RizzoliBooks
Pinterest.com/RizzoliBooks
Youtube.com/user/RizzoliNY
Issuu.com/Rizzoli

Yours,
London Lynn

Dear London Lynn

Well you fucked up big time didn't you? There is a reason
why everyone says you should always travel light. That said,
if you are truly innocent of any wrong doing and were simply
getting yourself confused with Lady Gaga then you need to
hire a good immigration lawyer and appeal your deportation.
Either that or accept your fate which I do NOT recommend.
Because if you accept your fate you will never experience
the frisson of seeing the Statue of Liberty for the first time
nor will you swoon over the New York skyline. You will miss
standing on glass, looking down open mouthed into the chasm
that is the Grand Canyon. You will miss driving through the
vast flat plains of the Midwest, through endless swaying
cornfields and you will never experience the sheer thrill of
lying on your back in the desert, high as a kite looking up
at the stars. You will never know what it feels like to be
pulled through the thick snow of Montana on a dog sleigh and
you will never walk through the ancient magical majesty of
the Redwood Forests.
Seems like so much to give up on so early on in your life.
The boy situation is somewhat irrelevant by comparison.
Boys who don't want to change, adapt, or compromise to be
with you are already a waste of a sentence. Fuck that, they
are ten a penny.
But the wonders of the world, they are priceless and
irreplaceable. So go do something about your ban from
entering the USA.
Fight for wonder. Fight for joy!

-Yours truly in agony,
 Auntie Beat

Dear Shirley

Why do I struggle to actually like people? I mean, all
I want to do is listen to the Cats soundtrack on my own.

Thanks,
Maggie.

Dear Maggie

You struggle to like people because most people are
arseholes. The thing you have to remember though is the
fact that most people feel the same way about most other
people too. Everybody thinks everybody else sucks ass.
Do any of us start out this way? Well quite honestly we
are not. Children are rarely unlikeable and more often
than not, perfectly delightful. So what happens between
childhood and adulthood that turns us all into raging
arseholes?
Oh let me count the ways! Disappointment, betrayal, loss,
loneliness, failure, rejection, and more disappointment.
Pain, fear, anger, hurt, confusion, frustration ,
indignation, outrage, revulsion, horror, and more pain.
Need I go on? I think not.
My point being, everybody has been dealt a shit sandwich.
There isn't a person you will meet who has not suffered. Not
one person who has had it easy. Not really. Not even the
people who look like they got it all. They didn't.
The next time someone is an asshole, try to remember
that they too are hurting. And when you remember that,
your compassion will come in to play. Suddenly it is much
easier to tolerate their bullshit, their bragging, their
self centeredness or their cruelty. So practice kindness
towards others….even when they don't deserve it. Your
practice of kindness will serve your own flagging spirits.
Elevate YOUR mood. Lift YOU up. Unless of course they are
being a completely off the charts arsehole in which case
you need to use your words and nothing BUT your words to
eloquently but mercilessly STAMP THAT SHIT OUT. Believe
me, when you do, it will MAKE YOU feel SO much better
about EVERYTHING.

Yours truly in agony,
Auntie Beat

your-if.
Meanwhile this brings us to your current situation. I just
don't think you are that into your new dude. Otherwise I
think you'd be saying something like, "I know my man is
balding but he's hot like Oscar Issac," or, "He is losing
his hair but he get's me. I mean he really, REALLY gets
me and he makes me feel good whenever he's around," or
something to that effect.
So chin up, dump him then strap on some high heels and head
on out into the night. Sooner or later you will find the
guy who doesn't give two figs if he is taller or shorter
than you. He will just want to be with you. He will want
to walk in any direction with you. Want to understand you,
talk to you until the sun comes up, scratch your back
even when you are super grumpy and you haven't been very
nice. He will want to read the books you rave about, he
will check out the music you recommend, he will tolerate
your crazy family, surprise you with little notes hidden
in your underwear drawer. He will hold your hair when you
are vomiting and then he will lie with you on the cold
bathroom floor until dawn because he is worried you are
going to choke on aforementioned vomit. He really won't
give a shit if you are taller than him, with or without
high heels. Point of fact he will downright love it because
he is just wild about you and everything about you is just
PERFECT. And trust me, you feel the same about him.

Yours truly in agony,
Auntie Beat

garbage.com